PRAISE FOR *GLUTEN-FREE ON A BUDGET*

"*Gluten-Free on a Budget* is filled with simple, sensible, and mouth-watering recipes. Use it in good health without breaking the bank!"

—Marilyn G. Geller, CEO, Celiac Disease Foundation

"Chandice and Tana's passion for helping those living a gluten-free lifestyle shines through recipe after recipe in *Gluten-Free on a Budget*. Packed with wholesome, nutrient-rich recipes, this book is one that will not only nourish your family without breaking the bank, but teach you to value your own health in a bigger way."

—Vanessa Weisbrod, Executive Editor, Delight Gluten-Free Magazine

"If you're in the market for a flavor-packed and budget-friendly gluten-free cookbook, this is a must-read. It's filled with easy-to-navigate meal plans, shopping lists, helpful tips on how to stock your pantry, and so much more. Say good-bye to spending tons of money trying to be gluten-free. This book will keep you on budget and leave you with a vast array of delicious recipes the whole family will love!"

—Amie Valpone, Editor-in-Chief of TheHealthyApple. com

"Though eating gluten-free on a budget might seem impossible, *Gluten-Free on a Budget* proves that you can eat a decadent and enjoyable diet filled with old favorites sans gluten without costing an arm and a leg. Practical and very reader-friendly, Chandice and Tana completely break down the process of stocking your pantry and then crafting delicious meals that everyone in the family will love. Whether you're a newbie to the gluten-free lifestyle or a 15-year veteran, you're sure to get a lot of valuable and cost-conscious tips to eat well on a gluten-free diet!"

—Jennifer Fugo, author, speaker, and founder of Gluten Free School

"What Chandice and her mother Tana have accomplished with this book is amazing. It is chock full of fabulous cooking and money-saving tips, which for us GFers is definitely appreciated. The recipes are quick, easy to follow, and simply delicious. I c   !
Rhubarb Cr

—Jilly Lagasse, co-author of "The Gluten Free Table: The Lagasse Girls Share Their Favorite Meals" & "The Lagasse Girls: Big Taste Bold Flavor & No Gluten"; daughter of world-famous chef Emeril Lagasse

"Chandice and Tana have written a comforting cookbook with heart, filled with sage advice and wisdom and served with a side of homemade gluten-free apple pie. *Gluten-Free on a Budget* provides great advice for budgeting, stocking a pantry, and saving money, while still letting you eat healthy, enjoy homemade creations, and stay free from gluten. These diverse recipes are notated with easy-to-read and -understand ingredients and instructions, occasionally with the handy tip about purchasing the best-for-you products for the recipe. I can tell that they have worked hard to put together a book that contains their lifelong learnings about maximizing your grocery budget while still cooking and baking with spirit and providing your family with comfort foods that will keep you safe—and full!"

—Erica Dermer, Founder of Celiac and the Beast, free-lancer for Living Without's Gluten Free & More Magazine and SheKnows.com Food & Health Experts

"Sound advice which will keep your palate pleased and your pocketbook from being overtaxed. Excellent tips on cooking in quantity, favoring naturally gluten-free foods, and making your own fabulous, tasty treats, like Brazilian cheese bread."

—Lola O'Rourke, MS, RDN, Education Manager of Gluten Intolerance Group

"Whether you're new to gluten-free or a veteran, *Gluten-Free on a Budget* is a great tool to help you stock your pantry, manage the grocery store, and create delicious meals for you and/or your family. I especially love the meal planning & grocery list included. A must read!"

—Keeley McGuire of www.keeleymcguire.com, "Allergy Friendly Fun Lunch Boxes"

"Anyone who has visited the gluten-free section of a grocery store knows that these products can be costly. In their new book, *Gluten-Free on a Budget*, authors Chandice Probst and Tana Besendorfer offer suggestions to help maximize variety of diet while minimizing the impact on your pocketbook. One of the best? Make your own food. Probst and Besendorfer make it easy with recipes like Peanut Butter Bars, Sweet and Sour Chicken with Ham Fried Rice, Nut-Encrusted White Fish, and All-American Apple Pie. Grab your copy, prop it open to your favorite recipe, and start cooking!"

—Kyra Bussanich, The Food Network's Three-Time 'Cupcake Wars' winner and author of "Sweet Cravings: 50 seductive desserts for a gluten-free lifestyle" (TenSpeed)

"After years of advocacy in the celiac community, Chandice is bringing her gluten-free expertise to print with her new cookbook. Her budget-friendly tips, mouthwatering photographs, and easy-to-follow gluten-free recipes are sure to become a favorite resource in your gluten-free kitchen."

—Erin Smith, Founder of Gluten-Free Fun and Gluten-Free Globetrotter, Leader of the NYC Celiac Disease Meetup Group

"Chandice and Tana have done a fabulous job of answering the need for a useful cookbook for the gluten-free family. Not only does this book give tips everyone can use to cut costs, which is essential for a family who is trying to manage their budgets, but they also manage to present favorite classic recipes from regions, with easy-to-attain ingredients that won't be impossible to find in our pantries or favorite grocery store—not a small feat to accomplish in the gluten-free world. A must-have for your collection!"

—Nikki Everett, Founder, GF/AF Wellness Events

"The tips in *Gluten-Free on a Budget* will save G-Free eaters hundreds at the grocery store—and even better, they'll be eating delicious family-friendly recipes like Crepes with Sweet Cheese and Strawberries, Navajo Tacos, and Granny Smith Apple Crisp. American Flag Cookie Pizza and Cheeseburger Soup are the kinds of recipes that remind us that food should be more than delicious and nutritious; it should be fun. This book is definitely one to add to the kitchen collection."

—K.C. Pomering, G-Free Foodie

"When folks learn they have to eat gluten-free, they often think they must reinvent their eating entirely. But it's just not true! *Gluten-Free on a Budget* reminds us that habits such as buying in bulk, baking at home, and striving to eat more natural, whole foods, are good rules of thumb whether you're gluten-free or not. Chandice and Tana do a great job of demystifying the gluten-free diet with easy tips like these, and also share the homestyle recipes you've been craving, made in delicious new gluten-free ways."

—Jules Shepard, gfJules.com, author of "Free for All Cooking: 150 Easy Gluten-Free, Allergy-Friendly Recipes the Whole Family can Enjoy"; "The First Year: Celiac Disease and Living Gluten Free"; and "Nearly Normal Cooking for Gluten-Free Eating"

"Gluten-free foods are more available and tastier than ever before. Despite the vast improvements in the options for the celiac disease and gluten-sensitive communities, there's still some work to be done in the affordability department. *Gluten-Free on a Budget* offers a solution by bringing readers the perfect blend of delicious food that keeps taste buds satisfied without breaking the bank."

—Alice Bast, President and CEO of the National Foundation for Celiac Awareness (NFCA)

Gluten-Free on a BUDGET

Chandice Probst & Tana Besendorfer

Front Table Books

An imprint of Cedar Fort, Inc.

Springville, Utah

ISBN: 978-1-4621-1608-9

Published by Front Table Books, an imprint of Cedar Fort, Inc.
2373 W. 700 S., Springville, UT, 84663
Distributed by Cedar Fort, Inc., www.cedarfort.com

Library of Congress Control Number: 2014949041

Cover and page design by Bekah Claussen
Cover design © 2015 by Lyle Mortimer
Edited by Justin Greer and Rachel Munk

Printed in China

10 9 8 7 6 5 4 3 2 1

Printed on acid-free paper

CONTENTS

FOREWORD

By Tammy Credicott

National bestselling author of The Healthy Gluten-Free Life, Paleo Indulgences, *and* Make-Ahead Paleo
www.TheHealthyGFLife.com

There are few things more pleasurable in this world than delicious food and amazing people. And right here, in this book, you get both. How lucky are we?

Chandice and Tana have become my long-distance gluten-free family over the years, and the reason is simple . . . they are good people. And I'm quite sure that after reading *Gluten-Free on a Budget* and cooking some of the fantastic recipes, you will feel the love and support too. You see, you're not just browsing the pages of a quick-fix, churn-'em-out type of cookbook (you know the ones . . . jumping on the gluten-free wagon to make a buck?). No—you will be experiencing the recipes, tips, and insight from two of the best people you'll ever hope to meet. With kind hearts, generous natures, and creative palates, you can't help but fall in love with their down-to-earth charm and homestyle recipes that fill the tummy but don't drain the pocketbook.

Gluten-Free on a Budget is filled with authentic home cooking by folks that really "get" what great-tasting, family-friendly, gluten-free cooking is all about. They don't just talk the talk. They live, breathe, and share their healthy gluten-free lifestyles every day in their business and personal lives. Even better, they've collected all of that experience and poured it into this beautiful book filled with great recipes, practical tips, and tons of eye appeal through color photos!

Chandice and Tana have outdone themselves with *Gluten-Free on a Budget*. Perfect for gluten-free newbies, but inventive enough to inspire the GF veterans. It will fast become the most-used book in your kitchen. I'll be honest . . . I'm a lazy cook. I'm all about easy, yet healthy recipes that are safe for my celiac family but nourish us without breaking the bank. *Gluten-Free on a Budget* definitely fits the bill in my busy household, and I know it will for yours as well. So get in the kitchen and start cooking, my friends! Everything you need is right here.

INTRODUCTION

OUR STORIES

In 2008, after years of horrendous stomach pain that had landed me in the hospital more than once, I (Chandice) was diagnosed with celiac disease.

My journey was a long, hard one that I wouldn't wish on anyone. At a high school dance camp, I collapsed onto my hotel room bed from the most severe stomach pain I'd ever experienced. I thought, "This must be what it feels like when someone gets stabbed in the stomach." Our team's sweet bus driver took me to the ER where they did x-rays and tests. They determined that my intestines were just clogged and sent me home with high potency medicine to help, which it did, but only temporarily. A few years later—after I had been married only a short time—the same thing happened again. This time, however, the pain was so bad that I couldn't unfold from a fetal position. My husband rushed me to the ER and carried me in, cradled in his arms. They immediately gave me a pain reliever intravenously. It was so strong that I remember feeling like I was flying. This time doctors said it was just bad ulcers and sent me home with heavy narcotics to "ease the pain." By this time, I just assumed that daily stomachaches were a part of life as I had been having them since the age of 14.

Around this time, my mom told me that she realized she suffered from the effects of celiac disease and was doing remarkably better on a gluten-free diet. She encouraged me to get tested for celiac disease. When I went in for my tests, the doctor told me, "I promise you do not have celiac disease." He pushed on my stomach and instructed me to tell him when I felt pain. When I did, he told me that I was wrong. I was in shock! Was he really telling me that I didn't know what pain my own body was having? I wanted to leave then and there, but I also wanted my test results. He again assured me I didn't have celiac disease and sent me home letting me know he would call me when the results came back.

A week later at his office, the doctor said, "I want to apologize; I was wrong. You do have celiac disease." I was then told that I had to eat gluten-free for the rest of my life and then he sent on my merry way with no further instruction.

This didn't seem right to me. I immediately started a blog, GlutenFreeFrenzy.com, where I could share my thoughts, recipes, and fun, gluten-free giveaways (since I was shocked to find out how much gluten-free food cost and thought I probably wasn't alone). I also founded the Celiac Disease Foundation Arizona East Valley Chapter to provide myself and others with local support. For me, jumping head first into the celiac world was how I coped. Following my mom's amazing example and finding the positives about this life I now had to live were other coping methods for me. I finally found my purpose in giving back to my community through celiac disease awareness.

At the time of my diagnosis in 2007, my husband and I thought we were ready to start a family. To reduce the risk of infertility and miscarriage due to undiagnosed celiac disease, my doctor recommended that I be gluten-free for one year before trying to get pregnant. My body was still healing and I needed to let it continue to do that before creating new life. We were thrilled when I got pregnant a year, to the month, after my diagnosis. I was able to carry a healthy baby full term and we have been blessed with him and his brother as the light and life of our home since. We are excited to invite our first little girl into our home to balance the beautiful chaos of having two little boys under one roof.

Both my mom and I had experienced a range of symptoms before our lifestyle change that I am sure many of you have as well. Between the two of us, we endured symptoms ranging from headaches, horrific stomach pain, and a foggy brain to mood swings, anxiety, and neuropathy. We were so grateful to finally find an answer to our health problems that we embraced gluten-free living 100 percent from day one and have never deliberately cheated. It just isn't worth the misery it would bring to eat gluten, and we know it's the only true way to heal.

When I received my celiac disease diagnosis, I didn't know much about what it entailed. What I did know was that I was not alone. My sweet mom was not only ready to help me in anyway she could—as she had been gluten-free for a few months at the time—but she was also positive from the beginning, always reminding me, "At least we know what the problem is and how to fix it." I loved seeing her excitement at the challenge of converting all of our favorite recipes, especially when it came to our holiday treats. Growing up, our home was always known as the "Thanksgiving home" or the "Christmas breakfast" home and even the "Halloween party" home with everything centered on themed food. Right away my mom began telling me all of the ideas she had for how she could convert our favorite sugar cookies or my favorite green bean casserole recipe. Her positivity has always given me hope that we would be okay. I feel blessed to have been diagnosed around the same time my mom found out her problems with gluten. She has provided me with so much support and I love that we have each other through this journey—especially during the holidays! For my family and me, just living gluten-free wasn't an option. We were living on a student budget and needed to be wise about our grocery bill each month. This challenge encouraged my mom to help me take our recipes one step further and create them with limited means. She also taught me so much about using every bit of our leftovers, and my husband and I have learned the art of meal prepping and planning over the years.

We wrote this cookbook with the hope of creating a sense of family for those who don't have that support along their gluten-free journey. We want you to know that you are not alone. We understand that just going gluten-free isn't always an option. Learning the skills of living this lifestyle on a budget can be tough, but we are happy to embark with you on this exciting gluten-free journey that so many of us must call life.

Hugs,

Chandice and Tana

TIME IS MONEY: WASTE NOT, WANT NOT

"Time is Money" and "Waste Not, Want Not" are proverbial phrases both attributed to Benjamin Franklin in the 1700s, but they are still as applicable in today's world.

One of the first things you may notice about our recipes is that we don't use a premade flour blend. There are two main reasons. Number one: It may seem like using a flour blend would be more convenient, but in the end will likely waste more time and cause frustration. With a flour blend, you start with a purchase of individual flours, starches, leavening agents, and gum, and then you combine them in proportions listed in the flour blend. When you are finished making the blend you will have used all of some flours and starches and have unused portions of others; it will never work out in perfect amounts.

Let's say you do have a blend. At some point you will have a recipe that calls for 1 cup of gluten-free flour blend and you have a little more than ½ cup. This means you will have to stop and make up your flour blend again, and what if you don't have enough of one item to make up a batch of the flour blend? You don't have the formula to just add the individual items to your recipe, so now you will have to stop cooking and go to the grocery store. So why not just use the flour and starch as it is needed? Keeping them separated can also help your products last longer; you can keep the ones that need to be refrigerated or frozen separate from the ones that can be stored in the pantry. This way you just buy each one as needed because some will definitely stretch longer and others will be used faster. The second reason is addressed in "The Greatest Wealth is Health" section that follows.

Cooking on a budget isn't about the cost of food only. Cooking on a budget also includes spending time, using your resources wisely, and making use of everything. It seems like everyone is pressed for time, days are shorter, and there is more to do each day than ever before. Planning ahead to save time, using leftovers, and making meal prep a little quicker and easier will also help you with your budget. You will be less likely to throw your hands in the air and order take-out or stop at the nearest drive-through (something that can really wreak havic in your budget) when your meals are planned and the main ingredients are prepared. Also, when you make use of leftovers, none of your hard-earned money is thrown down the drain or out with the garbage. Here are a few ideas to get you through your week.

I love making a big Sunday dinner. Roast chicken with mashed potatoes, gravy, and buttered basil corn is one of our favorite meals. I always roast an extra chicken so I can use the leftovers during the week for Hawaiian Haystacks (make extra gravy on your Sunday dinner and reheat it with the chicken and you have the meal practically made), Chicken Salad, Southwest Corn Chowder, Wild Rice Soup, Chicken Pot Pie, Creamy Chicken Lasagna, Mesquite Chicken Pasta Salad, Chicken Stir-Fry, Chicken Fajitas, Chicken Enchiladas, or Chicken Avocado Quesadillas.

You can also cook a large beef roast on the weekend and use the leftovers for things like Beef Stew, Beef Stroganoff, French Dip, Shredded Beef Tacos, or Roast Beef Sandwiches.

Cooking ground beef in larger quantities also works well. Tacos are the meal I always start with because I like taco meat to be from the first cook, not reheated. We have a special way of doing tacos that everyone raves about. We never know how many we might have on taco night so I always fry several pounds. Sometimes we have a lot left over and other times only enough for one other meal. Some of the meals I use the precooked ground beef for are Easiest Ever Chili, Rich and Meaty Spaghetti, Lasagna, Taco Casserole, Cheeseburger Soup, Shepherd's Pie, and Beef Stroganoff.

Here are just a few recipes for using leftovers:

CHICKEN GRAVY

¼ cup cornstarch

1 cup chicken broth

1 cup potato water

1 Tbsp. chicken drippings

1 tsp. dried parsley

2 tsp. salt

pepper to taste

Mix starch with ½ cup chicken broth. Heat remaining broth, potato water, parsley, salt, and pepper to boiling. Lower heat and whisk in starch mixture. Continue whisking until thick and smooth. *Always keep leftover gravy to use in other meals!*

BASIL BUTTERED CORN

16 oz. frozen corn

½ cube butter

1–2 tsp. dried basil

Melt butter in a saucepan. Add corn and mix to coat. Add basil and cook, stirring occasionally until heated through.

CHICKEN STIR-FRY

½ onion

1 Tbsp. sesame oil

1 cup diced carrots

1 green pepper

2 cups broccoli florets

¼–½ cup gluten-free soy sauce

2 cups diced leftover chicken

¼ cup walnuts (optional)

Cut onion into chunky pieces and sauté in sesame oil until the pieces are still slightly crisp. Add carrots and continue sautéing until the carrots are cooked, but still slightly crisp. Cut green pepper into one-inch pieces. Add green pepper and broccoli to the carrots and onions. Add half of the soy sauce and cover to steam. Add cooked chicken and additional soy sauce, then cook until completely heated. Add the walnuts if desired and serve over brown rice.

CHICKEN FAJITAS

2–3 cups sliced leftover chicken

2 green peppers

1 red pepper

1 onion

1 Tbsp. butter

1 Tbsp. fajita seasoning

brown rice tortillas or corn tortillas

Cut peppers and onions into one-inch pieces and sauté in butter until soft. Add in chicken and sprinkle with seasoning. Serve in a tortilla topped with grated cheese and sour cream.

CHICKEN AVOCADO QUESADILLA

2 brown rice tortillas
pepper jack cheese
leftover chicken, diced
avocado, sliced

Butter one side of each tortilla and place one tortilla butter-side down in a skillet. Set stovetop to a medium heat. Slice cheese and place on the tortilla to melt, add diced chicken and sliced avocados. Place second tortilla on top, butter side up. Flip quesadilla and cook the other side. Cut into wedges and serve with salsa and sour cream.

FRENCH DIP

1 Tbsp. butter
leftover roast beef
au jus (see below)
gluten-free bun or roll, toasted
provolone cheese, sliced

AU JUS
2 cups beef broth
2 tsp. Worcestershire sauce

Melt the butter in a skillet. Add roast beef and au jus ingredients. Heat through. Remove roast beef from skillet with a slotted spoon and place on a toasted gluten-free bun or roll. Place cheese on top of hot meat and slice sandwich in half. Remove au jus from skillet and put in small cups for dipping.

THE GREATEST WEALTH IS HEALTH

You may wonder why there is not a gluten-free flour blend in this book. There are two main reasons; the first we discussed the section "Time is Money: Waste Not, Want Not." We will now address the second reason. (If the reasons were ranked in priority, this would be the number one reason.) Most books try to make their ingredient lists look short and their recipes easier by putting a gluten-free flour blend in the front of the book and using it as an ingredient (for example, 2 cups gluten-free flour blend), instead of listing the individual flour, starch, and gum used. In some ways this may be easier—and it certainly makes a recipe look less intimidating—but if a premade blend is created and used for recipes ranging from cookies to quick breads, and from yeast bread or pie crust, the blend has to err on the side of extra starch for the items that need to be lighter. This doesn't make for better recipes because each baked good needs a different weight, taste, and texture. Plus it certainly isn't best for your health. The starches used in gluten-free baking contain far less nutrients and are much more likely to wreak havoc on your blood sugar than the flours such as teff, sorghum, coconut, or almond. I prefer to use only the amount of starch it takes to make a recipe wonderful and add as much of the wholesome grains as possible. I demand great tasting food but I want it to be as nutritious as possible, even if it is a dessert.

I am not going to go into deep details about nutrition in the food you eat or how food is a medicine on your path to regaining health; there are many books available that go into those very details. I just want to arm you with a little information on the basics that I feel are most important. Let's discuss some things to avoid and some things to do, along with some basic information to help you understand why. When you know the whys you can decide what is most important to you and what things you'd like to learn more about. I am not a physician or a nutritionist—the information is my opinion and is based on the personal research I've done.

THINGS TO AVOID

- Hydrogenated oils/trans fats: They increase bad cholesterol and increase inflammation (which is linked to many other chronic diseases).

- High fructose corn syrup: Free fructose (not bound to glucose) goes directly to your liver turning on a process called lipogenesis, which leads to a fatty liver. Fatty liver contributes to pre-diabetes and type 2 diabetes. HFCS also contains other contaminants, such as mercury.

- Food coloring: Some food colorings have been banned for use in the United States while others remain, despite concern over the possible toxicity of them. Use natural food colorings like turmeric, beet juice, and spinach.

- MSG: A flavor enhancer. Some possible reactions are headaches, sweating, facial pressure, numbness, heart palpitations, chest pains, nausea, and weakness.

- Nitrates: A principal concern about sodium nitrite is a possible link to carcinogenic nitrosamines, cancer-causing compounds. It is thought that sodium nitrate may also increase your risk of heart disease, diabetes, Alzheimer's, COPD, and an increase in the frequency of migraines.

- GMOs (most corn and soy): GMOs are very controversial. I think the effects are still greatly unknown so it's better to be safe than sorry.

- Preservatives: Preservatives in food can be carcinogenic when digested. There is a possible link between preservatives and weakening heart tissue, behavioral changes, and breathing difficulties.

- Soy products: Soy contains isoflavones which can also act as an estrogen mimicker and block the hormone estrogen. Soy also contains goitrogens which may adversely impact thyroid function. (Note: Fermented soy does not have the same adverse effects.)

DO USE GOOD QUALITY FATS AND OILS

There are only three oils used throughout this book: coconut oil, olive oil, and butter. Coconut oil is a fabulous choice of a medium chain fatty acid, or MCTs. These MCTs are metabolized differently. They go straight to the liver from the digestive tract, where they are then used as a quick source of energy. Coconut oil can help increase your metabolism. Cultures in areas where high amounts of coconut oil are consumed also have low incidents of heart disease. Coconut oil is antibacterial and antimicrobial, which means it can kill bad bacteria, viruses, and pathogens, and may help prevent infections. Coconut oil has a variety of uses not only in cooking, but also topically as a body and face lotion, as a natural deodorant, make-up remover, and as a hair mask to increase moisture and create a beautiful shine. Use a high quality source of organic, extra virgin coconut oil. Olive oil is rich in monounsaturated fatty acids. Olive oil may help in reducing the chance of heart disease, high blood pressure, breast cancer, and stroke. Regular consumption can reduce inflammation, which is responsible for an array of other problems, and reduce oxidative stress. Coconut oil and olive oil are both plant sources of fat, but now let's talk animal fat because we use a lot of butter, whole milk, cream, and meat in this cookbook. Butter consumption started decreasing around 1960 when margarine started picking up steam. Since the early 1970s there has been an increase in rates of obesity, diabetes, and heart disease despite the fact that the average American's consumption of saturated fat has dropped. If we as a society are eating less of something that is supposed to be bad for our health then why isn't our health improving? I personally think the number one reason to use butter is because it tastes amazing and it makes everything it's in or on taste amazing too! But there are real health benefits too (yay!). Butter is high in vitamin A (helps thyroid and adrenal problems many people with celiac and gluten intolerance suffer from), CLA (positive effects on metabolism and anti-cancer properties), and vitamin E and K2. Don't worry about eating whole milk and cream because they both contain high amounts of fat. Fat works as a carrier. If the fat comes from a healthy, organic animal the fat it contains will be full of good things (like essential fatty acids) and it will help facilitate vitamin E, A, D, and K transport in your body. If animal fat is from a poor source (one that has been given chemicals, hormones, and antibiotics in large amounts), those undesirable things are also stored in the fat. You will feel better about eating a high fat meal or dessert occasionally if you know that you are reaping the benefits of healthy fat. The same principles apply to meat—beef, pork, and poultry. We always eat the skin of the chicken when it's from a high quality source. Buy organic, grass-fed meat, butter (with no added coloring, but annatto instead), cream, and raw whole milk or the best you can afford. Remember, good fat is not bad for you and fat doesn't make you fat. Eat high quality fats with nutritional benefits.

DO EAT VEGGIES AND FRUIT ABUNDANTLY

Your body will benefit tremendously from eating lots of fresh fruits and vegetables. They are loaded with vitamins and minerals; to get the broadest benefit, think of eating a rainbow in fruits and veggies every day. You must be aware that many conventional produce items are high in pesticide residue. The Dirty Dozen (and the clean fifteen) is a list of fresh produce containing the highest (or lowest) pesticide residue. This list is fantastic in helping to decide the high priority items to purchase organic and the items that have little benefit in buying organic (so you don't waste money on something that isn't needed). Make a copy of the lists and keep them in your wallet. As you shop, pull out the list and compare pricing on the high priority items to see if you can work purchasing organic into your budget. Here is the website for the lists: http://www.ewg.org/foodnews/list.php.

DO EAT WELL TO HEAL YOUR BODY

Many of the recipes in this book aren't meant for daily consumption. Because it's a gluten-free cookbook it contains many of the recipes people are looking for that aren't naturally gluten-free. However, the things you should be eating daily are usually gluten-free already. So when you do eat breads and sweets and treats, indulge (not gorge) in the moment and really find pleasure in the food, but only occasionally. You can also swap the less desirable plain white table sugar for a less refined sugar like raw or organic sugar. Even better would be to switch to honey or maple syrup, and another step better would be coconut palm sugar or green stevia.

There are many good foods that can really help you on your path to vibrant health. Most of them you already know, but here is one you might not be familiar with: bone broth. Making your own homemade broth is a great way to use leftovers to the very end and to save money. Because you are boiling down a chicken carcass or beef bones, you are getting all the added benefits of the bone marrow and gelatin, neither of which do you get from a store-bought beef or chicken stock. Bone broth contains valuable minerals in a form your body can easily absorb and it is also an anti-inflammatory. The gelatinous substance that is rendered aids in digestion and is very healing to the lining of your gut, something that is very important to those with celiac disease. Never, never, never throw away animal carcasses or bones! Always, always, always make bone broth. If you don't have time immediately, freeze the bones and make it later, but don't waste something that will contribute greatly to your health as well as your pocket book. It's so easy to make and so very good for you. Always use the highest quality bones possible. Here are the instructions:

Fill a large stockpot with pure filtered water. Add the bones, skin, and whatever is left into the pot. Add 1–2 Tbsp. apple cider vinegar. You can also add celery, carrots, and onion for extra flavor and nutrition. Add one onion (skin removed and cut in half), 2–3 stalks of celery (just cut in half or fourths), 2–3 carrots (unpeeled and cut in half) and 1 Tbsp. of real salt. Bring to a boil. Reduce heat and simmer for at least 12 hours. Skim off any foam that floats to the top. If you don't have time to watch over your broth, put everything into a crockpot and let it simmer for 24 hours. Cool the broth. Using a slotted spoon, remove all the bones and veggies. Strain broth through a mesh strainer to remove any bone fragments. Broth can be stored in the refrigerator for 3–4 days or frozen for later use.

Alternate: Try boiling the whole chicken, meat, bones, and all. After boiling for 1–2 hours remove the meat to use in other dishes. (It's a great way to have precooked meat on hand.) Continue simmering the bone broth as instructed above.

DO GET PLENTY OF SUNSHINE, REST, AND EXERCISE

We will make this section really short because, after all, this is a cookbook. Rest; your body needs time to recover from the daily grind it is put through. Create an environment that is conducive to sleep and take naps when you can. It doesn't mean you are lazy; it means you are smart. Plan time for daily exercise. Move your body as much as you can. Walk a few steps further in the parking lot and take the stairs instead of the elevator. Find activities that you love and do them with the people that you love. Get out and walk in the sunshine, because natural vitamin D is one of the best health benefits you can give to your body. Most of these things are free but their value is immeasurable.

Do live an abundant life. Celiac disease or gluten sensitivity does not have to be a cloud of gloom and doom. Enjoy every day, work hard, play plentifully, love deeply, and laugh heartily, because there is much to be thankful for. Maybe you've finally found an answer to health problems you have suffered with for many years in gluten-free eating. However, it can be disappointing when you find your new gluten-free options to be less than exciting, complete with strange tastes and weird textures. I hope to make gluten-free eating a pleasure for you and to arm you with recipes that the whole family will enjoy eating; recipes you can take to a potluck party and no one but you will know its gluten-free. It will be food so good that none of it will go to waste!

I've included "Tana's Take It Up a Notch Tips" with many recipes in this book, which you can incorporate whenever possible to take things up a notch nutritionally. Try them one at a time or jump in with all of them and really accelerate on your path to health.

GLUTEN-FREE BASICS AND CELIAC DISEASE 101

It is important to emphasize that living gluten-free is not for everyone. Going gluten-free shouldn't be given as a blanket statement to the general population. It is so important that people consult a doctor right away if they suspect they have celiac disease or problems with gluten. Find one who is knowledgeable in the field of celiac disease, non-celiac gluten sensitivity, or NCGS and food allergies. Currently, accurate results for celiac disease can only come while an individual is eating gluten regularly and in fairly large amounts. Therefore, it is not recommended that you start a gluten-free diet until you have been properly tested for celiac disease. A solid diagnosis can provide so much confidence and closure for those likely to quit the diet after being discouraged by it. Celiac disease should be taken very seriously; no one who has been diagnosed should for any reason cheat and eat gluten. For those who have done all of the testing and still can find no conclusive results, but know they feel better living gluten-free, listen to your body. You know it better than anyone. If you feel miserable when you eat a certain food, it is ok to make the choice to avoid it. However, do the proper celiac testing first.

So what is celiac disease? According to the Celiac Disease Foundation (a wonderful resource), "celiac disease is an autoimmune disorder that can occur in genetically predisposed people where the ingestion of gluten leads to damage in the small intestine. It is estimated to affect 1 in 100 people worldwide." There are over 300 symptoms associated with celiac disease so that can make diagnosis difficult.

What is non-celiac gluten sensitivity? The Celiac Disease Foundation states that "gluten sensitivity is a condition with symptoms similar to those of celiac disease that improve when gluten is eliminated from the diet."

In addition to a massive amount of wonderful information on www.celiac.org, you can also find a great symptoms and conditions checklist. It only takes a few minutes to answer and can be helpful for your doctor.

The Celiac Disease Foundation says that "gluten is a general name for the proteins found in wheat (durum, emmer, spelt, farina, farro, KAMUT® khorasan wheat, and einkorn), rye, barley, and triticale." Forms of gluten are hidden in many common foods including some you wouldn't expect like soy sauce, licorice, canned enchilada sauce, and even frozen vegetables. So you may be asking yourself, "What *can* I eat?" Thank goodness there are so many wonderful options out there that are naturally gluten-free! Fruits, vegetables, cheeses that aren't started on bread (some moldy cheeses are), meat, and nuts are all safe in their pure forms. As mentioned before, gluten has been found in something as simple as frozen vegetables and shredded cheese in the bag. This is because manufactures use gluten to keep food from caking together. Stick to the natural foods mentioned above that are minimally processed or unprocessed for your safety. Potatoes, rice, corn, and beans are also great options for carbohydrates that are gluten-free. For baking, there are lots of great flours that you can use, but the ones we prefer are listed in our pantry section.

Starting a gluten-free diet can feel overwhelming at times, but remember that there are so many food options out there to keep your body and taste buds happy.

If you are looking for good reading material on celiac disease and non-celiac gluten sensitivity, these are a few of the books that we recommend.

Gluten Freedom by Dr. Alessio Fasano

Celiac Disease: A Hidden Epidemic by Dr. Peter Green

Celiac and the Beast by Erica Dermer

Jennifer's Way by Jennifer Esposito

Real Life with Celiac Disease by Melinda Dennis

Living Gluten-Free For Dummies by Danna Korn

STOCKING YOUR BUDGET-FRIENDLY, GLUTEN-FREE PANTRY

The number one thing we get asked is, "How can you live gluten-free on a budget?" Here are some of the tips we feel are helpful in showing that living gluten-free on a budget can be rewarding while still tasting delicious! If you follow these tips and stock up on the pantry items we suggest for the recipes in this book, you will be well on your way to save all that "dough" you've been spending up until now.

Eat gluten-free naturally! This is the best advice we can give. It will save you the most money. In addition, it will also help your body perform at it's best from all of the natural, unprocessed vitamins, minerals, and nutrients it will be receiving. Remember, brown rice, sweet potatoes, quinoa, nuts and seeds, meat and dairy (in their pure form), and fruits and vegetables are all great options for creating delicious, nutritious meals.

Buy in bulk: We like to stock up on organic brown rice, quinoa, and a number of other naturally gluten-free products at Costco. In fact, their coconut oil is one of the least expensive we have found yet. Our favorite gluten-free flour blends for when we are in a hurry and just need those Pamela's Products pancakes can often be found much cheaper on Amazon than at your health food store. When shopping at your local grocer, be sure to ask for a case discount. It is usually 10 percent but can be more. Bob's Red Mill products case consists of only a few bags so you won't feel like you are buying enough for an army. You will save so much money by making just a few small changes in where and how you shop. It will amaze you!

Meal prep and plan ahead: Cut up fruits and veggies twice a week (we prefer Sunday and Wednesday) and then store them in containers in the fridge so that you always have a healthy snack or side to your meals all ready to go. This will help keep you from reaching for the junk food. Meal prep is great because you will have nutritious lunches on the go rather than feeling like you have to stop and buy your meals. This alone will save you big on your grocery/eating-out monthly bill. We like to prepare a big batch of gluten-free pancakes or breakfast burritos and freeze them for quick breakfasts. You can then easily pull out what you need and go.

Use your crockpot: You can make any cut of meat a fabulous creation in the crockpot. It is like a magic cooking tool! Putting a big batch of meat in your crockpot at the beginning of the week will ensure that you have lots ready to use throughout the week for recipes in this book. Another great thing about the crockpot is that overnight you can put dry beans (which are super cheap), cover with water, and sprinkle with salt, then have a great source of protein for all kinds of meatless meals. In addition to the crockpot recipes in this book, we recommend Stephanie O'Dea's crockpot cookbooks. They are fantastic and full of lots of gluten-free crockpot meal ideas.

Meatless Monday: Or Tuesday, just choose one day a week and go meatless from breakfast to dinner. This is a great way to give your intestines a little break from heavy digestion as well as cut some money on your next grocery trip. I think this once a week detox from meat actually feels great and encourages you to get creative in the kitchen by trying new veggies. We have found some great vegan blogs from doing this that we wouldn't have otherwise. Our only word of caution with this is to make sure you aren't replacing your meat with yucky, soy-based or "fake" meat alternatives. Just keep it natural and unprocessed when making your meat-free meals.

Make your own gluten-free goodies: We all know we need them so why not make them yourself? Make a big batch of cookie dough, make a few cookies, and freeze the rest for another day. Baked goods are some of the most expensive things you will find on your grocery receipt so shake it up a bit and become an expert baker. Your wallet will thank you.

So what does a budget-friendly, gluten-free pantry look like? Here is what we suggest. Remember that health is wealth and that by purchasing your gluten-free flours individually, you are actually saving more by using only what you need per recipe rather than using an all-for-one flour blend that is often higher in starches than it needs to be. Remember to store your flours in the freezer for maximum life span. As you can see from the list below, we save BIG by not stocking our pantry with unnecessary processed items and treats. We prefer to make them from scratch in bigger batches so there is enough to enjoy on the day of baking as well as later. By not buying prepackaged snacks and goodies, you will save more than you could ever imagine and will definitely have enough money for the items listed below. Just think, you could buy a bag of gluten-free cookies for nearly the same price as a bag of brown rice flour that can be used for months in different recipes!

Baking items: sorghum flour, almond flour, white rice flour, brown rice flour, coconut flour, teff flour, tapioca starch, potato starch, cornstarch, arrowroot starch, cornmeal, unflavored gelatin, xanthan gum, milled chia seed, psyllium husk, yeast, powdered buttermilk, cream of tartar, sugar, brown sugar, powdered or confectioner's sugar, baking powder, baking soda, molasses, mesquite powder, cocoa powder, chocolate chips, gluten-free vanilla, and almond and mint extracts.

Condiments, spices, and oil: Real salt, black pepper, paprika and smoked paprika, cayenne, cumin, onion salt, garlic salt, seasoned salt, ginger powder, cinnamon, allspice, nutmeg, parsley, basil, oregano, dill, rosemary, bay leaf, tarragon, lemon pepper, chives, minced onion and garlic, thyme, poppy seeds, chili powder, turmeric, honey, Tamari gluten-free soy sauce, apple cider vinegar, lemon juice, olive oil, maple syrup, balsamic vinegar, gluten-free Worcestershire sauce, and coconut oil.

Pantry items: peanut butter, peanuts, almonds, pecans, walnuts, sweetened condensed milk, canned tomatoes, tomato sauce, tomato paste, refried beans, red beans, artichokes, diced green chilies, pumpkin, pineapple, green beans, canned clams and salmon, certified gluten-free oats, brown rice pasta, brown rice, popcorn kernels, olives, canned baby shrimp, gluten-free pretzels, gluten-free crackers or bread crumbs, naturally sweetened strawberry jam (NO high fructose corn syrup), coconut flakes, mustard, Dijon mustard, dill pickles, pepperoncinis, and tomato juice.

We recommend using Bob's Red Mill gluten-free flours as they are more finely milled and work best in our recipes. They are also the most cost-effective. Another thing we highly recommend is using only Real Salt–brand salt. It is much better tasting and is the best salt for your body because it is unprocessed and full of minerals. See the next paragraph for more information. When it comes to certified gluten-free oats we love Gluten-free Prairie. They are grown in Montana in gluten-free fields and then harvested and processed in a dedicated gluten-free facility. They are also naturally hull-less so have been minimally processed and are never soaked or steamed.

You will notice in each recipe that calls for salt, we always mention Real Salt. Real Salt is made in Redmond, UT, and is unprocessed and unbleached. It is full of trace minerals, more than 60 to be exact. This wonderful brand is currently available in onion salt, garlic salt, and seasoned salt, as well as just the traditional flavor. These salts can be found at nearly every health food store as well as online at www.realsalt.com. If you absolutely can't find this brand of salt, we recommend Celtic Sea Salt or Himalayan pink.

SAMPLE WEEKLY MEAL PLAN AND GROCERY LIST

These meal plans are put together with the suggestion to go over our suggested pantry list and stock up on the recommended items. In starting with those basic things, you will have a great base for baking and cooking gluten-free. Keep in mind that all ingredients on the grocery list need to be gluten-free even if not specifically noted.

BREAKFASTS

Buttermilk Pancakes

Breakfast Burritos

Kid-Friendly Green Smoothies

Ham and Green Chili Quiche

Flaky and Sweet Danish

DINNERS

Roasted Chicken, Mashed Potatoes with Gravy, and Parsley Carrots

Hawaiian Haystacks

Individual 7 Layer Dip Bowls with Corn Tortilla Chips

Grandma Joyce's Tacos

Taco Casserole

Shepherd's Pie

Salmon Patties and Tartar Sauce with Roasted Red Potatoes

TREAT

Peanut Butter Delights

GROCERY LIST

½ gallon milk

1 cup buttermilk

1 pound of butter

raw baby spinach

2 dozen eggs

4 pounds of ground beef

1 package of bacon

4 oz. ham

2 whole chickens

2 cans of salmon

2 small bags of frozen corn

6 cup cheddar cheese

½ cup pepper jack cheese

corn tortillas (whatever you need for your family taco night plus 9–12 for taco casserole)

1 bunch of green onions

1 small jar of salsa

1 can refried beans

1 bag of tortilla chips

2 six-pack bags of brown rice tortillas

11 russet potatoes

4 pounds of red potatoes

1 small bag of baby carrots

1 bag of carrots

1 cup of brown rice

3 large onions

1 green pepper

1 bunch of celery

1 bunch of bananas

1 small bag of ice

1 head of lettuce

3 medium tomatoes

2 bags of hash browns

1 small jar of mayonnaise

1 cup half and half

PANTRY ITEMS

flours and starches: tapioca starch, potato starch, almond flour, sorghum flour, brown rice flour, coconut flour, and cornstarch

xanthan gum

baking powder

unflavored gelatin

gluten-free almond extract

tomato sauce

sugar

coconut oil

canned pineapple

shredded coconut

gluten-free crackers or bread crumbs

diced green chilies

olives

spices: chili powder, cumin, turmeric, sage, Real Salt, Real garlic and onion salts, black pepper, dried oregano, lemon pepper, and dried parsley

lemon juice

minced garlic

peanut butter

almonds

BENTO BOX LUNCHES FOR ALL & GLUTEN-FREE KIDS

I have to preface this section with my admiration for Keeley McGuire of keeleymcguire.com. She is my ultimate bento box mom idol and is the best gluten-free, allergen-friendly bento box blogger I have found. Her ideas are fantastic. From easy, fun ideas in a hurry to holiday-themed and more elaborate lunches, she really helps guide you through your gluten-free bento box journey. Her personality and sweet disposition only add to her wonderful site as you see the love she has for her family in every post. Be sure to check her out!

When asked to do a TV segment on gluten-free bento box lunches, I not only gave my favorite ideas for meals and making the food fun, but I also had to show the best ways for packing those tasty lunches. I also shared my recommendations for making your child's gluten-free, back-to-school lunchtime a success.

So where do you begin when packing gluten-free lunches for the littles? First things first—you need the right lunchbox. I have tried many of them and have found the ones listed below to be the best all around.

Go Green Lunchboxes are my favorite, because they are adorable and practical, with perfectly sized compartments, custom-fit lids, cute carrying cases, and even a stainless steel water bottle right in the lunchbox! Whenever I take mine out, at least two people ask where I got it. People are drawn to the design and cute carrying case that comes in so many designs; you can surely find one that fits your child's personality. The white board attached to the inside lid for writing notes to your little sweeties are an added plus.

Kids Konserve is a fantastic line that is reminiscent of a brown bag lunch. It is reusable, eco-friendly, and made from recycled cotton, which makes it the perfect bag for school lunches. I personally love the look of this set and think it couldn't be cuter in little hands as they head off to school. This is another one that comes with a stainless steel canteen for carrying water, which encourages the "reduce and reuse" motto at an early age. This set also comes with a cloth napkin; a food kozy sandwich wrap with velcro (which can also be used as a placemat); and two circle, 8-oz. stainless steel, leak-proof containers for packing lunch items. It comes in many designs and is BPA-, PVC-, phthalate-, and lead-free. To have the complete meal set, you can order the bamboo spork, which makes even the utensils eco-friendly.

Planetbox is a very popular sustainable lunch box; however, it is much more pricey. When people think eco-friendly bento boxes, Planetbox is one of the first that comes to mind. This is the ultimate bento box design with its adorable little compartments and canisters for little items or dips. Even the pickiest eater will be pleased to see that their food doesn't touch. The stainless steel design makes it durable and also dishwasher safe, which is great for mom and dad. Different magnet designs make lunch fun again. My little guys chose the Winter Wonderland (go figure, since we lived in Arizona at the time) and loved them. There is even a create-your-own set that you could easily add your child's food allergies or dietary needs on in dry erase marker as I've seen some parents do. Planetbox comes with a five-year guarantee and currently has many different lunchbox designs for whatever size you need.

Easy Lunchboxes by Kelly Lester are definitely the most affordable, bento box–style, reusable lunchboxes. They have a fantastic design and come with great color options for the lids so that you can change them every day. The carry cooler also comes in many colors making, it easy for you to find one that your child enjoys. My boys quickly opted for the bright orange design and have loved it. Some of the features of this brand include easy-open, kid-friendly lids, durable dishwasher-, microwave-, and freezer- safe, *plus* BPA/PVC/lead/vinyl-free design. These lunchboxes are a #1 bestseller on Amazon, and I know why. To finally be able to have a reusable lunchbox that doesn't break the bank makes living more natural, something that everyone can do. This company also offers cute mini-dippers, which make it easy to send dressings and smaller items with your child.

From Japan With Love is a fantastic all-things-bento site. They have everything from traditional bento boxes to picks, egg molds, and nori and sandwich cutters. All are BPA-free, which makes lunches safer for your kiddos. From Japan With Love helps you jazz up any lunch using the fun things they offer. This is the place I recommend for bento box accessories. I know that for my boys, making a hard-boiled egg into a bunny makes it more fun to eat. I imagine this goes for many other kids out there. Their mini flower cutters are great for transforming cut pieces of fruit and vegetables into something everyone in the lunchroom will want.

Now what to put inside those cute lunchboxes, right? The possibilities are endless, but remember that with gluten-free on a budget, the best way to save is to eat as naturally gluten-free as possible. Fruits, vegetables, good cheese and meats, and homemade treats will be your best bet. It is so easy to fill your cart with quick and easy lunchbox "fillers" that look fun but have little nutritional value and cost a fortune. Do your child's body and your wallet a favor and get creative with real food. There are so many great ideas out there for bento box lunches, from elaborate and themed for every holiday, to simple but sure to put a smile on any child's face. Because of this, I made a Pinterest board specifically dedicated to "fun food," and to this day, it is still one of my favorite boards to pin to. Check it out at www.pinterest.com/gfreefrenzy.

Here are some lunches and snacks that I recommend for kiddos and adults. Everything is intended to be gluten-free, even if not specifically noted. *Always* check your ingredients, including lunchmeats and cheeses, to make sure you aren't getting any hidden gluten.

- Flower-sliced or other mini cookie cutter–sliced fruits and veggies
- Gluten-free meat and cheese rollups
- Make-ahead mini pizzas
- Cornbread muffins with chopped hot dog inside
- Sandwiches in all different shapes. (We love cutting a natural PB and J into a circle and popping out the center with a mini circle cookie cutter and then sprinkling the top with just a few sprinkles so it looks like a donut.)
- Gluten-free ice cream cones with fruit and yogurt on the side for filling and making a nutritious ice cream cone!
- Leftovers! Talk about saving big; this is a great way to do that.
- Cheese and gluten-free cracker stacks
- Sweet or savory waffle sandwiches
- Walking tacos: Pack a bag of gluten-free corn chips and put chili or meat, cheese, lettuce, tomato, and olives on the side with a little packet of mild salsa, if they like it. The kids open the chips, dump everything in, and eat it right out of the bag. They will love it!
- Chilled pasta salads with a little protein and their favorite veggies
- Tuna or chicken salad and crackers
- Breakfast egg cups: Fill each individual muffin cup with one egg and then add some chopped breakfast meat and cheese. Bake it at 350 degrees until cooked through for an *easy* breakfast or lunch and any time.
- Corn tortilla quesadillas
- Pancake bites: Similar to the egg cups, but you make them by pouring prepared pancake mix into muffin cups, adding your favorite pancake add-ins (fruit, chocolate chips, etc.), and baking them at 350 degrees until a toothpick inserted comes out clean.
- Apple sandwiches: Instead of bread, use sliced apple rings smeared with PB and J. Then put them together for a tasty sandwich. Just make sure to soak your apple rings in a bit of lemon juice first so they don't brown.
- Antipasto kebabs: On kebab sticks, stack gluten-free hard salami, pepperoni, cherry tomatoes, olives, marinated artichokes, and cheese, or whatever other things you think your child will eat.
- On-the-trail lunch: Jerky, dried fruit, nuts (if your child is old enough to eat these safely), and a few chocolate chips to make your children smile.
- Nachos
- Homemade French toast sticks
- Toasted sandwiches on a sucker stick. Keeley did this by shapin grilled cheese into a heart and star, and they couldn't have been cuter!
- Mummy mini pizzas for Halloween
- Gingerbread man cutout sandwich for Christmas
- Salad in a jar: Start with layering the dressing and wet ingredients on the bottom, and then place your greens on top. When you're ready to eat, just shake and enjoy!

In addition to great lunchboxes and meal ideas, here are a few other things I suggest for back to school fun and success:

Awareness and advocacy books for kids. I love the idea of gifting your child and/or your child's teacher with a great book like *The Gluten Glitch* by Stasie John. This lets your child know they are not alone, and it spreads awareness by adding it to your classroom library. You never know how many other families could use this great book; however, the teacher may have just the person in mind to share it with.

Wear-it-loud-and-proud apparel that gives your child confidence in knowing they are one cool kid. They may have food allergies or celiac disease, but they are going to rock it in their new awareness shirt from places like celiacandthebeast.com. Her pink gluten-free, flag-topped cupcake or black skull and wheat gluten-free crossbones kids' shirts are adorable!

Allermates and Medimates make sharing your child's food allergies fun with their cool character bracelets.

If you are looking for something more sophisticated that also helps make taking meals on the go easier, I would suggest 6 Pack Bags. While they aren't cheap, they are an amazing investment for those who eat on the go regularly. You can get a cooler-type bag or something classier that is both attractive and practical. Their line of handbag-inspired meal systems is both your purse and cooler in one. Nobody ever needs to know you carry full meals, safe gluten-free snacks, and ice packs to keep it all cool inside your purse!

So as you can see, we are now bento-box obsessed! Besides school lunches, I am always finding an excuse for us to take our cute lunchboxes out. From movies to play dates, you better believe our bento box lunches are in tow!

FOOD STORAGE & EMERGENCY PREPAREDNESS

Are your gluten-free 72-hour kits ready? If not, we can help you with all that you need to be prepared for any kind of emergency. Our families are big on food storage and family preparedness. Preparing wisely was something we were both taught from a young age. We were told that something could happen at anytime that would leave you relying on your food store and/or 72-hour kits. I had a friend whose family was forced to live off of their food storage for months on end after her husband lost his job. She said that she was so grateful for the small steps she took in getting prepared because had they not had it, they don't know what they would have done. An emergency can consist of anything from loss of job to a natural disaster. These alone are scary, but not knowing if you will have any safe food in these situations would likely overwhelm you with fear. That's why we've created this list of the gluten-free food items for your 72-hour kit as well as some basic needs and information on long-term food storage. Be sure to triple check that all products you use are gluten-free. Also keep in mind that water is likely the most important thing you can have in an emergency. We recommend getting a single water filtration bottle like the one from Lifesaversystems.com. It is very pricey but removes all bacteria, viruses, cysts, parasites, fungi, and other microbiological waterborne pathogens without the use of chemicals like iodine or chlorine. In an emergency you could literally fill this bottle with the dirtiest water and still be able to drink it. We also recommend having some clean water on hand for places where even dirty water isn't readily available.

To keep your 72-hour kits up to date and fresh, make a family evening out of rotating the products in each person's backpack once a year. We always looked forward to this night when we got to eat the snacks inside and fill it with new ones. You can even make it a family challenge by splitting into two teams and seeing who can create the best meal with the contents inside the backpack. Talk about a family memory you won't soon forget!

These are gluten-free food ideas we recommend for your 72-hour kit. You can get creative depending on your tastes but this is what we include in ours.

- Canned tuna and chicken: Costco or Kirkland brands are great and affordable.
- Protein powder packets: We really like Bipro and Nutrasumma brands, but if you have an allergy to dairy, stick with Nutrasumma's pea protein line.
- Peanut Butter packets: Ready-made, like Justin's, and powdered options, like PB2
- Bars: Kind, Glutino, Larabar, and Nogii are our favorites that have a longer shelf life.
- Goldbaums Wonder Meals or Go Picnic meals
- Dehydrated hashbrowns: Idahoean brand work well.
- Chocolate and candies
- Pretzels: Glutino and Snyder have great gluten-free options.
- Granola: Bakery on Main, Udi's, and Purely Elizabeth work well.
- Single serve certified gluten-free oatmeal packets like Bakery on Main offers
- Real Salt & Pepper
- Jerky and nuts
- Bouillon cubes—Massel works well.

Gluten-free kids snacks: We love Qwackers, Envriokidz bars, Ella's Kitchen squeezable meals, Nogii kids bars, and Surf Sweets gummies.

When it comes to long-term food storage, the recommendation has been to start by buying extra pantry items that you use regularly and rotate them. If you buy canned green beans or refried beans, buy an extra few cans each time you go to the store then rotate the oldest to the front and newest to the back when storing. Always use the oldest first to keep your rotation up to date. Honey is excellent because it can last on your shelf for over 30 years when stored properly! Other items that can last 30 years on the shelf when properly packaged and stored correctly include white rice, dried pinto beans, dried corn, white sugar, potato flakes and non-fat powdered milk. Keep in mind that things like oil need to be rotated every 1–2 years at least.

This is a lot of information to take in for those who don't have any food storage or an emergency backpack. It can definitely feel overwhelming. Start small and get your 72-hour kits put together. Once that is done, move on to your everyday gluten-free pantry expansion. This will give you peace of mind that you have some food in your pantry alone to get you by if needed. Lastly, you can get those big items like the bucket of rice or dried pinto beans for your 30-year food storage. No matter where or how you start, you are on the road to being prepared with safe food in any emergency.

Here are some websites that are helpful for disaster preparation.

http://www.bt.cdc.gov/
http://www.ready.gov/
http://beprepared.com/
http://www.glutenfreeemergencykits.com

LIVING GLUTEN-FREE IN A GLUTEN-FILLED WORLD

As mother and daughter, we were so blessed to have started this new gluten-free lifestyle right around the same time. From the start, our families and spouses have been our biggest advocates so we have always had an amazing support system. However, we know this isn't the case with everyone. We have vowed to help others the same way so many have helped us. Time and time again we have heard horror stories of people who were deserted, either physically or emotionally, by loved ones after their celiac disease or non-celiac gluten sensitivity (NCGS) diagnosis. This is heartbreaking and we want to do everything we can to make sure that nobody feels alone on his or her new gluten-free journey. Thankfully there are many blogs, resources, and support groups out there to make this a reality.

Here are some things that we recommend once you begin your gluten-free lifestyle. Whether due to a celiac disease, NCGS, or a severe wheat allergy diagnosis please know that you are supported. Each is unique and different but all are equally regarded as a medical ailment that deserves the respect of those around you. Remember that you have this ailment but that it doesn't need to encompass who you are. You are so many other wonderful things other than just your disease. Remembering this will help you stay positive and see the good that has come from your diagnosis.

FIND A SUPPORT SYSTEM

There are so many resources both online and in person. There are multiple support groups around the nation that have monthly meetings and events. Here are some of our favorite national organizations:

The Celiac Disease Foundation (CDF) is our personal favorite. Their national education conference is fantastic! Learn more about them at www.celiac.org

National Foundation for Celiac Awareness (NFCA) is a fantastic online support resource that we consider another favorite. They often have webinars, chats, and events, which are very helpful. Find out more about them at www.celiaccentral.org

National Celiac Disease Society is a wonderful non-profit organization that is dedicated to raising funds for youth with celiac disease through its one-of-a-kind scholarships. You can visit them at www.celiacnation.org

Gluten Intolerance Group—www.gluten.net

Celiac Sprue Association—www.csaceliacs.org

Delight Gluten-Free Magazine, *Gluten-Free Living* magazine, and *Simply Gluten Free Magazine* are excellent print and digital resources for those living gluten-free. For those with extensive food allergies, *Living Without's Gluten Free and More* magazine as well as the magazine *Allergic Living* make fantastic resources.

Bloggers are fun and often provide much-needed humor and understanding. There are so many wonderful blogs full of fantastic recipes and stories, as well as product, book, and restaurant reviews. Gluten-freeFs or gluten-free friends can make the difference between an enjoyable gluten-free life and one that is constantly plagued by burden and despair. I have been so blessed to have the greatest gluten-free friends that make my journey not only one that is doable, but also one that is fun! We celebrate this lifestyle together and know that come what may, we will always be here for each other. We will continue to give it our all, 100 percent of the time because when you have celiac disease, eating gluten-free 99 percent of the time just doesn't cut it.

DECONTAMINATE

In addition to eating gluten-free, you must also avoid cross-contamination in every respect. This will require you to either have a 100% dedicated gluten-free kitchen (which most cannot do and don't have) or to lay some serious ground rules. Let's start with the basics. A dedicated gluten-free toaster, colander, utensils, sponges, cutting board and so on are going to be required to keep you from getting sick. If you must have gluten in your house, have a dedicated cupboard and preparation area for it. Glutenfreelabels.com *rocks* and makes it easier for a family to know which peanut butter jar is gluten-free and which one isn't, for example.

Whether you choose to use their labels or some of your own, make sure you are diligent in labeling things.

For your bathroom, makeup and hair care products as well as lotions, toothpaste, and medications can all contain gluten and quite often do. Switch all products out with gluten-free versions. We love Red Apple Lipstick brand for cosmetics. They are all 100 percent gluten-free and come in a great variety: from eye shadows and lipstick to fantastic mascara. Some people ask why gluten-free makeup and body care is necessary. It's true that you must ingest gluten for it to be a problem, unless you have a skin condition known as dermatitis herpetiformis or DH—then even skin surface gluten contact can cause a reaction. The problem comes when you are constantly using products on your skin and hair that contain gluten, over time you are likely to ingest some by touching your body or hair and then not washing your hands before you eat. Over the span of a lifetime, most women ingest a sickening amount of lipstick and lip-gloss simply by licking their lips. So even if you don't change anything else about your beauty regimen, we highly recommend that you change what you put on your lips. Remember, cross-contamination comes in many forms and that includes kissing—yes kissing. Have your spouse or significant other be mindful of what they eat and when they kiss you. Either they will prefer to just eat gluten-free or they will be brushing with safe toothpaste a lot!

TAKE CHARGE

This is a lifelong change that you are making and you must be your own advocate. Those who allow a little gluten here and there make it so tough for those of us who try to explain over and over that even a crumb is harmful. It is very hard when friends have heard, "Yeah, I have celiac disease but I can cheat every once in a while." *No*, we absolutely cannot, and we must change that mindset. When you are grocery shopping, be meticulous about reading labels. When in doubt, don't buy it. The *Is That Gluten Free* app makes grocery shopping easier. *The Essential Gluten-Free Grocery Guide* by Triumph Dining is another fantastic resource when shopping. It is best to stick to clean, whole foods whenever possible. Eating naturally gluten-free will be the best thing you can do to heal damage that has been done over the years to your body while you were eating gluten before receiving a diagnosis. It is also the cheapest way to live gluten-free.

When dining out, be sure to always call ahead and speak to the chef. Ask every question you can about preparation, cross-contamination, and the gluten-free menu offerings. Since the whole staff is part of your dining experience, it is also important that you feel comfortable with everyone from the server to the chef, as well as the manager's knowledge of preparations for those with celiac disease or serious food allergies. It may seem dramatic but we recommend letting the server, chef, and manager know that even if gluten is cross-contaminated with your food, you will be violently ill before even leaving their restaurant as well as for weeks to follow. Whether you have this severe a reaction or not, it will make them take note and truly pay attention to your food preparation. Resources like the *Find Me Gluten Free* app and the *Can I Eat Here* website are great for helping you locate a safe place to dine no matter where you are.

BE PREPARED

Always carry safe snacks that you can dive into when you are out. It is better to be safe than sorry and many times you will find yourself with nothing to eat if you haven't planned ahead. Enzymes and Redmond Clay help if you have been "glutened" despite your best efforts. Many people with celiac disease often have other food allergies and intolerances, including those to dairy and corn. If you are still not feeling better after following the above tips, talk to your doctor about what options for food allergy testing are available to you.

It is important to surround yourself with people who are willing to support you. Don't allow anyone to bully you into eating gluten. It is not worth it! This is a complete life change, so be patient with yourself as you find ways of navigating your new gluten-free world. You are strong. You can do this!

great starts

BISCUITS AND SAUSAGE GRAVY

BACON, SPINACH, AND TOMATO FRITTATA

CREPES WITH SWEET CHEESE AND STRAWBERRIES

FLUFFY BUTTERMILK PANCAKES

HAM AND GREEN CHILI QUICHE

JUMBO BLUEBERRY MUFFINS

PEANUT BUTTER CHOCOLATE CHIP MUFFINS

RASPBERRY CREAM CHEESE MUFFINS

RASPBERRY TOASTER PASTRY

FLAKY AND SWEET DANISH

OATMEAL PANCAKES WITH BUTTERMILK SYRUP AND FRIED APPLES

KID-FRIENDLY GREEN SMOOTHIE

HASH BROWN BREAKFAST CASSEROLE

BOMB BREAKFAST BURRITOS

BISCUITS AND SAUSAGE

GRAVY

Biscuits and gravy are a Southern classic, but I remember making them at the first restaurant I worked at. Fluffy biscuits and thick, rich sausage gravy were the favorites of the local farmers. This hearty breakfast will take you well past lunchtime. —Tana

INGREDIENTS

SAUSAGE GRAVY

½ lb. sausage

2 cups whole milk, divided

3 Tbsp. cornstarch

½ tsp. Real Salt

½ tsp. black pepper (optional)

Buttermilk Biscuits (p. 136)

 INSTRUCTIONS

Brown sausage (or use leftover sausage from another recipe) in a skillet. Remove browned sausage from pan; leave a tablespoon or two of drippings in pan.

Combine ½ cup milk and cornstarch. Pour remaining 1½ cups milk in skillet and heat, adding salt and pepper. Whisk milk with cornstarch into the hot skillet milk. Cook until gravy thickens and then add browned sausage. Split biscuits in half and serve with gravy on top.

TANA'S
TIPS
TAKE IT UP A NOTCH

Pork is generally cured and preserved with nitrates; take it up a notch with nitrate-free sausage.

BACON SPINACH

TOMATO FRITTATA

A fritatta, or an Italian egg cake, is similar to an omelet or a crustless quiche to which you can add a variety of meats, cheese, and vegetables, and so on. Frittatas are a fast and beautiful way to add flare to otherwise ordinary egg dish, and let's face it; it's really fun to say frittata! It makes you feel like a gourmet chef. —Tana

INGREDIENTS

8 oz. bacon

8 eggs

salt and pepper to taste

1 large tomato, sliced thin

1 cup spinach

4 oz. cheese, grated
(I use pepper jack)

 INSTRUCTIONS

Preheat broiler. Fry bacon to lightly crisp. Reserve 1 tablespoon bacon grease. Whisk together eggs, salt and pepper. Coat oven-safe skillet with reserved bacon grease, pour beaten eggs into pan, and heat at medium. Let eggs cook until center is wet, but not runny, lifting edges to let eggs to flow underneath.

Add tomato slices, spinach, and bacon. Continue cooking for a couple minutes. Top with cheese. Remove to broiler for 3–4 minutes until cheese is melted and lightly browned.

Organically raised, pasture-fed chickens produce eggs with yolks that are a deep orange color—no pale yellow yolks here. You can literally see the nutritional difference and your taste buds will be happy you took it up a notch!

Nº 36 CREPES WITH SWEET CHEESE

TANA'S **TIPS** TAKE IT UP A NOTCH

If fresh berries aren't in season, thaw 3 cups of frozen berries and add sugar. You can serve it this way or blend together and make a soft fruit jam.

AND STRAWBERRIES

I have always loved staying in a bed & breakfast that served crepes for breakfast. Unfortunately I've never found one that serves gluten-free crepes. So on weekend mornings when I want to be a little fancy, I make up a batch of these beautiful, paper-thin, gluten-free crepes. The most amazing thing is that they hold together so you can wrap sweet cheese and berries in them and serve them looking just as amazing as those at the bed & breakfasts. —Tana

INGREDIENTS

CREPE BATTER

2 tsp. brown butter

2 Tbsp. brown rice flour

2 Tbsp. coconut flour

2 Tbsp. tapioca starch

1 Tbsp. sorghum flour

1 Tbsp. potato starch

½ tsp. gelatin

¼ tsp. xanthan gum

1 Tbsp. sugar

¾ cup whole milk

2 Tbsp. water

3 eggs

additional 3–4 Tbsp. whole milk

SWEET CHEESE

½ cup cottage cheese

¼ cup sour cream

1 oz. cream cheese, softened

½ cup powdered sugar

BERRIES

3 cups sliced strawberries

⅓ cup sugar

 INSTRUCTIONS

In a small saucepan, brown butter and remove from heat. In a mixing bowl, combine all dry ingredients together. Add to the cooled butter ¾ cup milk, water, and eggs. Mix well. Add wet ingredients to dry ingredients a little at a time until batter is well blended. Put in the refrigerator and chill for 30 minutes. Remove from refrigerator and stir in 3–4 tablespoons milk. Batter should be very thin. Lightly grease a crepe pan or medium frying pan. Heat the pan over medium heat until it is hot. Lift it from the burner and pour in a couple tablespoons of batter (more depending on the size of your pan) in a circular pattern. Quickly swirl the pan to cover the bottom with a thin, even layer of batter. Put the pan back on the stove and cook until the crepe is lightly browned. Carefully flip the crepe with a spatula and brown the other side. Remove from pan and repeat with remaining batter.

In a blender add cottage cheese, sour cream, and cream cheese. Blend together well. Remove from the blender and mix in the powdered sugar until no lumps remain and cheese is smooth.

Combine berries and sugar together and let sit briefly.

Run a thick line of sweet cheese down the center of the finished crepe, place a few berries on the sweet cheese, and roll up. Top with additional berries and a dusting of powdered sugar.

FLUFFY BUTTERMILK

PANCAKES

When I make these pancakes on a Saturday morning, I always think of the Jack Johnson song, "Banana Pancakes." Sometimes I even listen to it while I'm making them. Now I know these aren't banana pancakes but they are really light, fluffy buttermilk pancakes which is the epitome of this song (I can't picture him eating flat, heavy pancakes and singing the song). This is how your weekend should start—with light, fluffy pancakes and not waking up too early. But, even if it's not the weekend, you can make these pancakes anyway and pretend like it is. —Tana

INGREDIENTS

⅓ cup almond flour

⅓ cup brown rice flour

¼ cup sorghum flour

⅓ cup tapioca starch

1 Tbsp. coconut flour

¼ tsp. gelatin

½ tsp. xanthan gum

½ tsp. baking soda

2 tsp. baking powder

2 Tbsp. sugar

2 Tbsp. butter

1 cup buttermilk

¼ cup milk

2 eggs

 INSTRUCTIONS

In a stand mixer, combine all dry ingredients and mix well. Melt butter, add buttermilk and milk, and whisk in eggs. Blend the wet ingredients into the dry ingredients. A little more milk can be added if needed, but the batter should be fairly thick.

Heat skillet or griddle to a medium/high heat. Using an ice cream scoop, scoop batter onto hot pan. Use the back of the scoop to spread out the batter a little bit. Let the pancakes cook until the edges appear done and it is nicely browned. Flip the pancake and cook the other side. Avoid patting the pancake down or flipping it multiple times; this will decrease the fluffiness. Enjoy with your favorite topping.

TANA'S TIPS TAKE IT UP A NOTCH

Use real maple syrup on your pancakes. The flavor is amazing and it doesn't contain all the unhealthy ingredients that are in imitation syrup.

HAM AND GREEN CHILI

QUICHE

I love a good quiche, but I would probably love any quiche because I love eggs. I chose this particular combination because I always have some ham in the freezer and the green chilies are canned, so they are really easy to keep on hand. Plus I love the spicy kick of green chilies and pepper jack cheese. Quiche is such a versatile dish, you can literally open your refrigerator and select any veggies that are starting to look a little sad, combine them with a little meat, and throw them in a quiche and you have an amazing breakfast, brunch, lunch, dinner or late night snack. Quiche works any time; you don't need a special occasion. Don't be afraid to try new combinations; just go for it. —Tana

INGREDIENTS

6 eggs

1 cup half & half

4 oz. ham, diced

1 (4-oz.) can diced green chilies

1 cup shredded cheddar cheese

½ cup shredded pepper jack cheese

3 diced green onions

½ tsp. Real Salt

¼ tsp. pepper

1 unbaked pastry crust (p. 224)

 INSTRUCTIONS

Preheat oven to 350 degrees. Whisk eggs well. Then add half & half and continue whisking until well blended. Add all other remaining ingredients. Pour into an unbaked pastry crust. Bake for 40 minutes.

Additional quiche ideas: asparagus and bacon, broccoli and sausage, mushroom and onion, spinach and ham.

TANA'S **TIPS** TAKE IT UP A NOTCH

Make a couple crusts in advance and freeze them to make this dish quicker to prepare, or make a crustless quiche.

JUMBO

BLUEBERRY MUFFINS

Nothing beats warm homemade blueberry muffins straight from the oven with lots of butter. They are heavenly for breakfast, brunch, or snacking. These easy-to-make muffins are soft, fluffy, and full of blueberries. For this recipe I make them in a jumbo size, but you can make them in the size that is best for you. —Tana

INGREDIENTS

¼ cup butter

1 cup brown sugar

2 eggs

1 tsp. gluten-free vanilla

½ cup vanilla yogurt

½ cup whole milk

1 tsp. lemon juice

⅓ cup almond flour

½ cup brown rice flour

¼ cup sorghum flour

3 Tbsp. coconut flour

½ cup tapioca starch

½ cup potato starch

4 tsp. baking powder

½ tsp. xanthan gum

1½ –2 cups blueberries, fresh or frozen (thawed and drained)

 INSTRUCTIONS

Using a stand mixer, cream together butter, sugar, eggs, and vanilla. Add yogurt, milk, and lemon juice. Combine all dry ingredients and mix well.

Add dry ingredients at a little at a time to wet mixture. Mix until well blended. Let stand for 15 minutes.

Heat oven to 375 degrees. Fold in blueberries to distribute evenly throughout batter. Using an ice cream scoop, scoop batter into greased jumbo muffin tins. You can use paper liners if you want. Bake for 24–25 minutes or until a toothpick in the center comes out clean. Makes 6 jumbo muffins.

TANA'S TIPS TAKE IT UP A NOTCH

Cultured dairy works so nicely with gluten-free flours. It helps in breaking down the flours and adds a nice moist texture. Use an organic full fat vanilla yogurt.

PEANUT BUTTER

CHOCOLATE CHIP MUFFINS

Peanut butter and chocolate are the perfect combination, and now you can have this perfect combination for breakfast, or serve it with a nice cold glass of milk to have a great midmorning snack. I took these muffins to a potluck BBQ thinking it was a strange contribution, but I had been taking pictures for this book and didn't have time to make anything else. I certainly didn't want to come empty-handed or bring something store-bought. I laid them out with the spread and offered my apologies for this random addition to the host. I was happily surprised when the muffins were the first thing to disappear and everyone was commenting on how good they were; most people had no idea they were gluten-free. So apparently they aren't just for breakfast and snacking, they work well at BBQs too! - Tana

INGREDIENTS

⅓ c. almond flour

½ c. brown rice flour

¼ c. sorghum flour

3 T coconut flour

½ c. tapioca starch

½ c. potato starch

4 tsp. baking powder

½ tsp. xanthan gum

1¼ c. brown sugar

2 T butter

2 eggs

1 tsp. vanilla

1½ c. vanilla yogurt

1 c. whole milk

⅔ c. peanut butter

1 c. chocolate chips

 INSTRUCTIONS

Using a stand mixer, cream together butter, sugar, eggs, and vanilla. Add the peanut butter, yogurt, and milk. Combine all dry ingredients and mix well. Add the dry ingredients a little at a time to the wet mixture. Mix until well blended. Let stand for 15 minutes. Heat oven to 375 degrees. Fold in the chocolate chips to distribute evenly throughout batter. Spoon batter into a greased muffin tin. You can use paper liners if you want. Bake for 18–20 minutes or until a toothpick in the center comes out clean. Makes 12 muffins.

RASPBERRY CREAM

CHEESE MUFFINS

It is a wonderful surprise when you bite into a muffin and it's filled with a creamy raspberry cream cheese filling. Make a big batch; you might not be able to eat just one. —Tana

INGREDIENTS

¼ cup butter

1 cup sugar

2 eggs

1 tsp. gluten-free vanilla

½ cup vanilla yogurt

½ cup whole milk

1 tsp. lemon juice

⅓ cup almond flour

½ cup brown rice flour

¼ cup sorghum flour

3 Tbsp. coconut flour

½ cup tapioca starch

½ cup potato starch

4 tsp. baking powder

½ tsp. xanthan gum

CREAM CHEESE FILLING

4 oz. cream cheese

⅓ cup powdered sugar

1 Tbsp. milk

raspberries

INSTRUCTIONS

Using a stand mixer, cream together butter, sugar, eggs, and vanilla. Add yogurt, milk, and lemon juice. Combine all dry ingredients and mix well. Add dry ingredients at a little at a time to wet mixture. Mix until well blended. Let stand for 15 minutes.

Heat oven to 375 degrees. Prepare cream cheese filling by combining all ingredients and whisking until smooth. Put cream cheese mixture into a ziplock bag and snip a piece off the corner. Grease a muffin tin.

Using a small spoon or scoop, put a small amount of batter in the bottom on the cups. Pipe cream cheese on top of the batter. Place a few raspberries in the cream cheese. Cover with another small scoop of batter, making sure to cover cream cheese and berries completely. Bake for 16–18 minutes. Let muffins cool completely. Any extra cream cheese can be piped on muffin tops.

RASPBERRY

👉 INSTRUCTIONS

In a saucepan, combine all filling ingredients and heat on a medium heat, stirring frequently. Cook until raspberries are hot and mixture has thickened. Remove from heat and set aside.

Preheat oven to 400 degrees. Using a stand mixer, combine the first nine dry ingredients; mix well. Remove butter from freezer and grate ½ cube at a time into dry ingredients. Lightly fluff in butter as you go. After all the butter is grated in, mix a few turns until all butter is coated in the flour mixture.

Add buttermilk, vinegar, and 2 tablespoons of beaten egg with a stir or two in between each one. Add ice water one tablespoon at a time. Mix together until dough sticks together and is a nice smooth texture. Roll out dough immediately or place in refrigerator. Dough should be slightly colder than room temperature when you roll it out, but not refrigerator cold. Place plastic wrap on the counter surface.

Divide dough in half. Roll dough into a large rectangular shape. Using a pizza wheel, cut dough into

TOASTER PASTRY

Can you remember the last time you had a Pop Tart? Pop Tarts aren't very good for you, but sometimes they taste really good. Some gluten-free options have come out on the market, but they are not all I expect in a toaster pastry. After coming up with an amazing pastry recipe, it only made sense to turn it into a toaster pastry. These are so delish warmed up and it's a quick easy breakfast or snack with a nice cold glass of milk. —Tana

3 × 5 rectangles. After cutting dough, lift the plastic wrap edges and invert dough into your hand. Place on a baking pad or parchment lined cookie sheet. Leave enough space in between each pastry that you can work around it. Get a small bowl of water to dip your fingers in.

Place 3–4 tablespoons of raspberry filling on each pastry, spread to the shape of the pastry leaving ¼ inch around all edges. Dip your finger in the water and run it around the edge of the pastries. Roll the other half of dough as directed and place on top of the filled pastries. Using the tines of a fork, seal the edges of each pastry. Make a few decorative holes in the top for venting.

Lightly brush the tops (not edges) with remaining egg. Bake for 17–19 minutes or until golden brown. Pastries can be eaten immediately, stored in the refrigerator for a few days, or frozen to use later. For icing, combine powdered sugar and milk; mix until smooth. Place in a ziplock bag, snip a small piece from the corner and squeeze on in a pattern of your choice. Ice pastries when ready to eat (do not ice before toasting).

INGREDIENTS

RASPBERRY FILLING
- 10 oz. frozen raspberries
- ½ cup sugar
- 3 Tbsp. cornstarch

PASTRY
- ¼ cup brown rice flour
- ½ cup white rice flour
- ½ cup tapioca starch
- ½ cup arrowroot starch
- ½ tsp. xanthan gum
- ½ tsp. gelatin
- ½ tsp. Real Salt
- ½ Tbsp. buttermilk powder
- 1 Tbsp. sugar
- ½ cup butter, frozen
- 1 Tbsp. buttermilk
- 1 egg, beaten (set aside 2 Tbsp.)
- ½ Tbsp. apple cider vinegar
- 1½–2 Tbsp. ice water

ICING
- 1 cup powdered sugar
- 1–2 Tbsp. milk

FLAKY

AND SWEET DANISH

This Danish is literally to die for! My friend Ashley first introduced me to her version before I got diagnosed with celiac disease. I was so smitten by her out-of-this-world dessert that we just had to convert it to a gluten-free recipe. Thank you, Ashley, for introducing us to this lightly sweetened dessert. —Chandice

INGREDIENTS

**FLOUR BLEND
(2 cups total):**
½ cup tapioca starch
½ cup potato starch
⅓ cup brown rice
flour
⅓ cup almond flour
⅓ cup sorghum flour
1 tsp. xanthan gum
1 tsp. baking powder

BASE LAYER
½ cup butter
1 cup gluten-free
flour blend
2 Tbsp. water

ALMOND ICING
2 cups powdered
sugar
1 tsp. almond extract
milk (just enough to
make a thick glaze
after sugar and
almond extract are
combined)

EGG LAYER
½ cup butter
1 cup water
1 tsp. gluten-free
almond extract
1 cup gluten-free
flour blend
3 eggs

 INSTRUCTIONS

For the base layer, cut small pieces of butter into the flour mixture. Sprinkle water over and combine gently with your hands. Gather the pastry and press into an 8 × 8 pan.

For the egg layer, heat butter and water to a rolling boil; remove from the heat. Quickly stir in the almond extract and flour. Return to low heat and stir vigorously with a wooden or plastic mixing spoon (no metal) until mixture forms a ball, about one minute. Remove from heat. Add eggs one at a time and beat with spoon until smooth and spreadable.

Spread over the base layer and bake at 350 degrees for 50–60 minutes or until topping is crisp and golden brown.

Cool pastry, then top with icing. Sprinkle with slivered almonds.

NO 52 OATMEAL PANCAKES WITH BUTTERMILK SYRUP AND FRIED APPLES

These pancakes are one of the most addicting things we have ever eaten. Year after year we receive requests to make them for all 40+ people at our annual family Lake Powell trip. Once you have had them, you think about them often. You dream about when you will make them next and you savor every bite when you do. Hey, and did you know that you can make buttermilk using just regular milk and lemon juice? We enjoy doing this to save money. —Chandice

INGREDIENTS

CERTIFIED GLUTEN-FREE OATMEAL PANCAKES

2 cup certified gluten-free oats

2 cup milk

2 Tbsp. lemon juice

2 eggs

¼ cup butter

2 Tbsp. sugar

1 tsp. baking soda

1 Tbsp. cinnamon

½ tsp. salt

FRIED APPLES

2 Granny Smith apples

2 Tbsp. butter

1 Tbsp. sugar

1 tsp. cinnamon

BUTTERMILK SYRUP

½ cup butter

¾ cup sugar

½ cup milk

1 Tbsp. lemon juice

1 tsp. gluten-free vanilla extract

1 tsp. baking soda

 INSTRUCTIONS

For pancakes, take ½ cup of oats and ground finely in a blender until they are coarse flour. Add that to the remaining oats in a large bowl. Mix the milk and lemon juice in a glass. Allow to rest for five minutes, and then stir and add to the bowl of oats. Mix well and refrigerate overnight. The following morning, add the remaining ingredients and mix well. Cook on a preheated, well-oiled griddle in small amounts.

Slice the apples thin and then fry in butter with sugar and cinnamon until just starting to soften.

For syrup, mix the milk and lemon juice in a cup and let rest for 5 minutes. Combine that with the butter and sugar in a pot over medium heat and bring to a boil. Remove from heat and add the vanilla and baking soda. Serve hot over oatmeal pancakes.

TANA'S TIPS TAKE IT UP A NOTCH

Use organic apples and coconut palm sugar; it tastes fantastic in the fried apples.

KID-FRIENDLY GREEN SMOOTHIE

Everybody wants their kids to eat their greens, but sometimes that can be more of a dream than a reality. With these tasty green smoothies, the kiddos will be eating a heap of raw, vitamin-rich spinach and will thank you for letting them! —Chandice

INGREDIENTS

1½ cups milk or milk alternative (almond milk, coconut milk, etc.)

5 cups raw baby spinach

2 Tbsp. peanut butter or other nut butter

16 drops liquid vanilla stevia, OR ¼ cup sugar

2 bananas

2½ cups ice

2 scoops gluten-free protein powder (optional)

 INSTRUCTIONS

Combine all ingredients in a blender and mix on high until completely blended. Enjoy cold.

TANA'S TIPS TAKE IT UP A NOTCH

Use fresh organic spinach for the kiddos.

HASH BROWN BREAKFAST CASEROLE

We make this casserole for nearly every special breakfast where extended family will be joining us. It's easy and it's a crowd pleaser. You can get creative and add what you like, including diced green chilies, tomatoes, and peppers. —Chandice

INGREDIENTS

1 (32-oz.) bag gluten-free hash browns

6 eggs

2 cups shredded pepper jack or cheddar cheese

1 lb. gluten-free sausage

1 tsp. Real Salt

½ tsp. black pepper

 INSTRUCTIONS

Preheat the oven to 350 degrees. In a 9 × 13 pan, melt 1 Tbsp. butter in the oven. Remove; then add the hash browns. In a frying pan, crumble and cook the sausage until no longer pink. In a bowl, whisk the eggs, salt, and pepper. Sprinkle the sausage over the hash browns and the eggs over that.

Top with the cheese and bake at 350 degrees for 40–45 minutes or until a knife inserted comes out clean.

BOMB BREAKFAST BURRITOS

These are so easy to make and are especially great for meal prep. Make a double or triple batch and individually freeze them in a double layer of tin foil and a freezer ziplock bag for later use. With these, it's so easy to pull out one or more at a time and heat them up for a delicious and nutritious breakfast. —Chandice

INGREDIENTS

2 Tbsp. coconut oil

1 (32-oz.) bag gluten-free hash browns

8 eggs

1 cup shredded cheese of your choice

2 tsp. Real Salt

1 tsp. black pepper

butter for tortillas

brown rice or corn tortillas

 INSTRUCTIONS

In a large skillet, heat the coconut oil to hot but not smoking. Add the hash browns and half the salt and pepper. Cook until golden brown and just starting to get crispy. Flip then cook until your liking.

In a bowl, whisk the eggs and pour into another frying pan. Scramble the eggs with the remaining pepper and salt as well as the cheese. Once cooked, add to the hash browns. Turn off heat and cover with a lid to keep warm.

Smear a bit of butter on both sides of a tortilla and in the empty egg frying pan, cook 1–2 minutes on each side until soft and golden. Put some hash brown mixture on each tortilla then roll up and enjoy. You can also roll them by in a double layer of tin foil and freeze for later use.

soups, salads, sides, and little bites

ARTICHOKE DIP

MOM'S FAMOUS CHEESE BALL

SEVEN-LAYER DIP

MOM'S CABBAGE SALAD

TEMPURA VEGETABLES

POTATO CAKES

CHICKEN SALAD

MESQUITE CHICKEN PASTA SALAD

CREAMY POTATO SALAD

WATERGATE SALAD

CHEESEBURGER SOUP

CREAMY RICH CLAM CHOWDER

CREAM OF CHICKEN SOUP

CREAMY TOMATO SOUP

DEBBIE'S FAMOUS HAMBURGER SOUP

EASIEST CHILI EVER

SOUTHWEST CORN CHOWDER

ARTICHOKE

DIP

Artichoke Dip is always on the menu for our annual New Year's Eve party and Thanksgiving appetizers. It also makes a great quick and easy potluck pleaser. —Chandice

INGREDIENTS

2 (15-oz.) cans artichoke hearts

2 (4-oz.) cans diced green chilies

1 cup mayonnaise

1 cup Parmesan cheese

 INSTRUCTIONS

Drain artichokes and then mash. Add green chilies, mayonnaise, and cheese. Mix together thoroughly. Bake at 350 degrees for 35–40 minutes. Serve with gluten-free tortilla chips, crackers, or veggies.

TANA'S TIPS — TAKE IT UP A NOTCH

Take it up a notch with mayonnaise that is free of soy. Soybean oil is very commonly used in this condiment, but beware: most soy is GMO. Look for mayo that uses grapeseed oil, sunflower oil, or another healthy oil as the base.

This cheese ball is a must at all family gatherings. We actually have to make two because they go so fast! It is delicious with gluten-free crackers or veggies. For Halloween fun, we even turned this recipe into a "Frankencheese." —Chandice

INGREDIENTS

2 (8-oz.) pkgs. cream cheese

1 cup shredded cheddar

1 tsp. lemon juice

½ tsp. onion, minced

1 tsp. garlic salt

1 tsp. chives

1 Tbsp. parsley

1 Tbsp. mayonnaise

1 (4-oz.) can baby shrimp, drained OR 1 pkg. gluten-free bacon, cooked and chopped + 1 Tbsp. bacon fat

⅔ cup chopped pecans or walnuts (substitute gluten-free pretzels for those with nut allergies)

 INSTRUCTIONS

Mix everything together except the nuts. Once combined, roll cheese ball in nuts and refrigerate overnight.

SEVEN-LAYER DIP

Whether you choose to make this in individual serving or as one larger dip to serve at a party, it is sure to be a crowd pleaser. Each layer of flavor, when combined, marry perfectly. —Chandice

#61

INGREDIENTS

1 (15-oz.) can refried beans

1 cup salsa

1 cup guacamole

½ pint sour cream

1 cup shredded cheddar cheese

2 roma tomatoes

1 cup olives, sliced

½ cup diced green onions

 INSTRUCTIONS

Combine the beans and salsa in a bowl and then layer it in the bottom of your pan or individual serving glasses. Carefully spread guacamole over the beans and the sour cream on top of that. Sprinkle the cheese on top and then add the tomatoes. Finish with the olives and green onions. Serve with gluten-free tortilla chips.

MOM'S

CABBAGE SALAD

This is one of our family's favorite recipes. It is one of those recipes you will try once and never forget! This dish is quick and easy, yet full of flavor and so delicious. It takes less than 15 mintues to make and makes an excellent accompaniment to any meal year round. While it is fancy enough to serve at a formal bridal shower, it isn't too pretentious to serve at a family picnic. —Chandice

INGREDIENTS

1 pkg. gluten-free bacon

1 head purple cabbage, chopped into strips

1 cup gluten-free feta cheese

1 cup walnuts, chopped

3 Tbsp. balsamic vinegar

Real Salt to taste

 INSTRUCTIONS

In a large pan cook the bacon until crisp and then transfer to a plate and cool. Add the cabbage to the bacon grease. Cook until slightly tender. It should still be a bright purple. If you overcook it you will lose the vibrant color and be left with a brownish cabbage.

Add balsamic vinegar, chopped bacon, and as many walnuts as you prefer and toss lightly. Transfer to a serving plate and top with feta cheese and salt to taste.

TANA'S
TIPS
TAKE IT UP A NOTCH

Try a naturally cured nitrate-free bacon—Beelers brand is my favorite.

POTATO

CAKES

I'm a farm girl, I grew up eating plenty of potatoes and I still love them cooked in many ways. Many times extra baked potatoes get thrown away because we don't know what to do with them. Making potato cakes is one great way to use them up. It is quick and easy and adds a little flair to your morning fare! —Tana

INGREDIENTS

1 cup cooked, shredded potatoes

1 egg, beaten

½ cup grated cheese

1 Tbsp. potato starch

½ tsp. Real Salt

¼ tsp. pepper

1–2 tsp. chives or green onions (optional)

1–2 Tbsp. coconut oil or butter for frying

 INSTRUCTIONS

Combine all ingredients. Heat oil in a skillet. Form into patties and place in hot oil, frying on first side until the potato cake is sufficiently browned before flipping it to the other side.

Note: You can use frozen hash browns if you want to make these when you don't have leftover baked potatoes. Thaw them first.

CHICKEN

SALAD

Chicken salad is a great summer meal. It's quick and easy to make and is a great way to use leftovers from a baked or rotisserie chicken meal. Add it to your next picnic fixings or pack it in a lunch. It always hits the spot. —Tana

INGREDIENTS

1 lb. (2 large breasts) chicken, cooked and diced

1 cup red grapes

2 green onions

2 celery stalks

⅓ cup salted nuts, chopped (I prefer almonds or cashews)

DRESSING
½ cup sour cream

½ cup mayonnaise

½ Tbsp. Dijon mustard

½ tsp. dill weed

1 tsp. honey

½ tsp. Real Salt

¼ tsp. pepper

INSTRUCTIONS

Combine all the sauce ingredients in a bowl and mix well. Cut the grapes in half; dice the green onions and celery. Combine chicken, grapes, onions, and celery.

Pour the dressing over the top and mix until everything is well coated. Add the salted nuts.

TANA'S
TIPS
TAKE IT UP A NOTCH

If you eat as much chicken as I do, going with an organic, free-range bird is important. Some of the benefits besides nutrition that you will notice with organic free-range chicken are a firmer textured and a more flavorful meat. It is also on sale more frequently than most other types of meat.

MESQUITE CHICKEN

PASTA SALAD

I having been making this family favorite salad for nearly 20 years. I tried it at a community function and decided I need to make my own version. Converting it to gluten-free was an easy exchange of the pasta noodles. No worries, we can enjoy it for another 20 years, just gluten-free. —Tana

INGREDIENTS

1 lb. chicken, cooked and diced or shredded (use leftover)

24 oz. gluten-free penne pasta

10 oz. frozen corn, thawed

½ green pepper, diced

½ red pepper, diced

¼ purple onion, diced

1 (15-oz.) can sliced black olives

DRESSING

1 Tbsp. seasoning salt

½ Tbsp. Real Salt

1 tsp. sugar

¼ tsp. cornstarch

¼ tsp. dried parsley

1–½ tsp. mesquite powder

1–½ tsp. smoked paprika

⅛ tsp. cayenne

⅛ tsp. white pepper

⅛ tsp. cumin

⅛ tsp. ginger

½ cup olive oil

⅛ cup apple cider vinegar

INSTRUCTIONS

Cook pasta according to manufacturer's directions, drain and cool. Add chicken, corn, peppers, onion, and olives, and toss together. In a bowl combine all dry dressing ingredients; mix together. Add olive oil and vinegar, whisk together until well blended. Pour dressing over pasta mixture and toss to coat. If the pasta sits in the refrigerator and dries out a bit, add a little more olive oil to moisten it. The dry mixture can also be used as a rub on grilled chicken.

TANA'S TIPS TAKE IT UP A NOTCH

Mesquite powder and smoked paprika will go a long way; look for them in the bulk bins, in very small packages or split them with a friend.

TEMPURA VEGETABLES

Tempura vegetables are one of those dishes that most living gluten-free have yet to enjoy. Tempura is typically made using wheat flour, so this recipe is exciting, as it brings back an old favorite in a safe way.
—Chandice

INGREDIENTS

¼ cup tapioca starch

¼ cup potato starch

¼ cup brown rice flour

¼ cup white rice flour

⅔ cup club soda

1 egg

½ tsp. Real Salt

coconut oil for frying

tempura vegetables (broccoli, cauliflower, carrots, etc.)

 INSTRUCTIONS

Heat the oil until very hot but not smoking. Mix the flours and salt together with a fork. Slowly mix in the egg and club soda. Make sure not to over mix. Dip the vegetables into the batter and fry 5 minutes or until the crust is golden brown and the vegetables are starting to soften.

CREAMY POTATO SALAD

The grilled onions really take this potato salad to the next level. I had a friend who never liked potato salad taste it and say it was definitely the best she had tried. I'm telling you, the key is those delicious grilled onions. —Chandice

INGREDIENTS

6 medium red potatoes

⅔ C mayonnaise

2 T yellow mustard

4 boiled eggs, diced

1 tsp. Real Salt

1 tsp. pepper

1 medium onion, diced

1 T butter

½ tsp sugar

½ tsp Real Salt

2 T Dill relish

½ tsp. smoked paprika

 INSTRUCTIONS

Cut the red potatoes into small 1–2 inch cubes, and then boil until soft but not falling apart.

Meanwhile, place the butter in a large frying pan over medium heat. Once it is melted, add the onions and ½ teaspoon each of salt and sugar. Cook until onions begin to soften and get some brown color.

Drain the potatoes when they are cooked and place in a large bowl. Add the onions and remaining ingredients and mix to combine. Once combined, feel free to add a bit more of any ingredient depending on your personal taste preference.

WATERGATE

SALAD

Watergate is one of the few gelatin-type salads I like, but then again it's not really a gelatin; it's a pudding, right? With homemade pistachio pudding and real whipped cream it's a salad that is more dessert than salad. But I think we should just call it a green salad; now you can eat all you want. —Tana

INGREDIENTS

PISTACHIO PUDDING

2 cups heavy cream

2 cups whole milk, divided

¾ cup sugar

2 Tbsp. butter

¾ cup finely ground raw pistachios

½ cup sugar

4 egg yolks

6 Tbsp. cornstarch

1 tsp. almond extract

2 cups whipped cream

2 (20-oz.) cans crushed pineapple, drained

1 cup chopped nuts (pecans or walnuts work best)

INSTRUCTIONS

In a medium saucepan, combine cream, 1 cup milk, ¾ cup sugar, butter, and ground pistachios. Heat until butter is melted and milk is slightly scalded. As the pistachios are cooked they will release their green color.

Whisk together egg yolks and ⅓ cup sugar. Slowly add this mixture to the hot mixture, whisking lightly. Continue cooking for 10–15 minutes on a low heat until mixture starts to thicken a bit. Mix reserved milk and cornstarch together. Add to the hot milk mixture, whisking constantly. Intermittently whisk as mixture continues to cook for the next 5–10 minutes.

When pudding has thickened remove from heat and blend in almond extract. Cover with plastic wrap (to avoid skimming) and place in refrigerator to cool. When pudding is cold, add pineapple and nuts. Fold in whipped cream and serve.

SOUP

This soup is like a cheeseburger and fries in a bowl. All the best flavors make it a favorite of even the pickiest soup eaters. It's hearty enough to stand as a meal all on its own and will warm up the coldest winter nights. —Tana

INGREDIENTS

½ to 1 lb. ground beef, cooked and drained (use leftovers)

½ cup diced onion

½ cup shredded carrots

2 Tbsp. butter

4 cups diced peeled potatoes

4 cups home-made beef broth (page 12)

1 tsp. dried parsley

½ tsp. garlic

1 tsp. Real Salt

½ tsp. pepper or ¼ tsp. cayenne for spicier

¼ cup cornstarch

1 cup whole milk

8 oz. grated cheddar cheese

¼ cup sour cream

INSTRUCTIONS

In a large saucepan melt butter and then add onion and carrots. Sauté until tender. Add beef broth and potatoes, bring to a boil. Simmer for 15 minutes until potatoes are tender. Add ground beef, parsley, garlic, Real Salt, and pepper.

Combine milk and cornstarch, and mix until smooth. Gradually add to hot soup mixture, stirring continually. Bring to a boil for 2 minutes or until thickened and bubbly.

Reduce heat; stir in cheese until melted. Remove from heat and blend in sour cream. Serve with additional cheese and chives.

CREAMY RICH

CLAM CHOWDER

This clam chowder is thick and filling. It has a creamy texture full of tender chunks of potato and lots of delicate clams. The flavor is delicate and mild, but if you like a spicier version, a little pinch of cayenne will give it some kick. —Tana

INGREDIENTS

2 (6½-oz.) cans chopped clams

1 cup minced onion

1 cup minced celery

2 cups diced potatoes

1½ tsp. Real Salt

1 bay leaf

¾ cup butter

6 Tbsp. cornstarch

1 cup water

2 cups whole milk

2 cups heavy cream

black pepper to taste

INSTRUCTIONS

Drain the juice from clams; reserve clams and juice separated. Put potatoes, onions, celery, salt, and bay leaf in a medium stock pot. Pour the clam juice over the vegetables and add just enough water to barely cover them.

Simmer over medium heat until all vegetables are tender. Add in butter and melt. Reduce heat and add in milk and cream; heat through. Whisk cornstarch into the water. Slowly pour into the chowder mixture, whisking as you pour in.

Add in the clams and black pepper and/or cayenne if you prefer. Let the chowder continue to simmer and thicken, stirring occasionally. Makes 8 bowls.

TANA'S TIPS TAKE IT UP A NOTCH

Instead of regular black pepper, grind fresh peppercorns into your clam chowder. It adds an amazing flavor!

CREAMY TOMATO

SOUP

Sometimes I like a simple soup that is smooth and creamy. This soup is worth a little effort because it is so much better than a canned tomato soup. Combine it with a grilled cheese sandwich and you have a marvelous meal. Freeze any leftovers and save for another quick and easy meal. —Tana

INGREDIENTS

½ c. butter

1 c. minced onions

1 c. minced carrots

1 c. minced celery

1 lg. can crushed tomatoes

2½ c. tomato juice

3 c. chicken broth (use your own homemade)

1 tsp. basil

1 tsp. tarragon

1 tsp. thyme

1 tsp. dill weed

1 tsp. minced garlic

1 c. heavy cream

INSTRUCTIONS

Sauté onions, carrots, and celery in butter until tender. Transfer to a stock pot and add the remaining ingredients except the cream. Simmer for 10–15 minutes, stirring occasionally. Add cream and heat through. Using a submersible blender, blend soup until smooth. Alternate: Working in small batches, transfer soup into a blender and blend until smooth.

TANA'S TIPS TAKE IT UP A NOTCH

Use tomatoes and tomato juice that come in glass jars or bottles. The BPA lining can leach in highly acidic foods.

CREAM OF CHICKEN SOUP

This is a staple in many homes for cooking. With cream of chicken soup, casserole and crockpot recipe options are endless. The only problem is when you can't eat gluten; the only canned options are quite pricey. With this, you can turn your favorite recipes into gluten-free options again! —Chandice

INGREDIENTS

3 cup homemade gluten-free chicken broth (page 12)

1 cup milk

½ cup butter

¼ cup cornstarch

½ tsp. black pepper

1 tsp. Real Onion Salt

1 tsp. Real Garlic Salt

½ tsp. tumeric

½ tsp. sage

 INSTRUCTIONS

In a stockpot, heat chicken broth and butter over medium heat until just starting to boil. In a pitcher or cup with a spout, combine the milk and cornstarch with a whisk. Gently pour into broth, making sure to whisk briskly.

Once thoroughly combined, add spices and continue whisking often. Let the soup simmer until thickened then serve hot with fresh parsley on top or use as needed in other recipes. You may freeze for later use.

DEBBIE'S FAMOUS HAMBURGER SOUP

My mother-in-law knows that I just adore when she makes this soup. I can eat three bowls in one sitting! This soup is great because again, you can use leftover meat if you have it and the process of simmering everything together makes it full of flavor. Thanks, Mama Debbie, for this great recipe. —Chandice

#81

INGREDIENTS

2 lb. ground beef

1 onion, diced small

1 (46-oz.) can tomato juice

46 oz. water filled in the tomato juice can after pouring juice out

3 Tbsp. sugar

3 Tbsp. parsley

2 Tbsp. chopped green pepper

3 Tbsp. salt

1 Tbsp. black pepper

2 cup diced potatoes

3–5 medium carrots, peeled and chopped

¾ cup chopped celery

¼ cup dry rice

INSTRUCTIONS

If not using leftover beef, brown the meat with the onion and drain. Combine all ingredients and simmer 3–5 hours over low heat.

CHILI EVER

Would you like to have dinner ready in 5 minutes? You can do it with this chili; it can be put together in less than 5 minutes and when you arrive home that night you will be treated to a hot and hearty meal. It pairs very well with the honey sweet cornbread or the cheesy jalapeño cornbread and a big glass of cold milk. —Tana

INGREDIENTS

1 lb. ground beef, cooked (use leftover)

1 (15-oz.) can tomato sauce

1 (15-oz.) can diced tomatoes

1 (4-oz.) can diced green chilies

2 (15-oz.) cans red beans (with juice)

3–4 Tbsp. chili powder

1 tsp. dried minced onion

1 tsp. minced garlic

1 tsp. Real Salt

½ tsp. garlic salt

INSTRUCTIONS

Dump everything into a crockpot and mix together. Cook on low for 6–8 hours.

CORN CHOWDER

This south-of-the-border soup is sure to become a family favorite. It's quick and easy to make, especially when using leftover chicken. Topped with crispy tortilla strips, it will feel like your own little fiesta! —Tana

INGREDIENTS

1½ lb. chicken, cooked and shredded or diced (use leftover)

½ cup onion, diced

1 tsp. garlic, minced

3 Tbsp. butter

2 cups chicken broth (page 12)

1 (4-oz.) can diced green chilies, undrained

1 (15-oz.) can diced fire roasted tomatoes, undrained

1 tsp. cumin

1 tsp. Real Salt

1 (10-oz.) pkg. frozen corn, thawed

3 cups cream

2 cups shredded pepper jack or Monterey Jack cheese

fresh cilantro

crisp tortilla strips

1 pkg. brown rice tortillas

Real Salt

coconut oil

INSTRUCTIONS

In a large stock pot, melt butter. Add onions and garlic, and sauté until onions are clear and tender. Add cooked chicken, chicken broth, tomatoes, green chilies, and spices.

Using a blender, blend 1 cup cream and half (5 ounces) of corn together to make creamed corn. Add to the soup along with the remaining corn and cream; heat through (but don't boil). Add the cheese and stir in. For the tortilla strips, slice or cut the tortillas into thin strips. Heat ¼ inch coconut oil in a large skillet. Cut tortillas into thin strips.

Place the tortilla strips in a single layer in the hot oil. Fry until lightly browned, flip and fry the other side until lightly browned. Remove from oil and sprinkle with Real Salt. Repeat, adding more oil as necessary until all tortillas are cooked. Top soup with tortilla strips and cilantro.

TANA'S TIPS TAKE IT UP A NOTCH

Use sprouted brown rice tortillas; they work really great for frying because they are already a little sturdier.

☞ *the main event*

CHICKEN POT PIE

CHICKEN TIKKA MASALA AND NAAN BREAD

DUTCH OVEN POT ROAST WITH ROOT VEGETABLES

HAWAIIAN CHICKEN

NUT-ENCRUSTED WHITE FISH

CRISPY CRUST PIZZA

ROASTED CHICKEN & BRUSSELS SPROUTS

SALMON PATTIES AND TARTAR SAUCE WITH RED ROASTED POTATOES

SHEPHERD'S PIE

SWEET & SOUR CHICKEN WITH HAM FRIED RICE

SWEET & SPICY PORK ROAST

THREE-CHEESE WHITE SAUCE LASAGNA

INSIDE-OUT BURGERS AND HOMEMADE POTATO CHIPS

CROCKPOT RIBS AND TWICE-BAKED POTATOES

CREAMY ITALIAN CHICKEN

TACO CASSEROLE

GRANDMA JOYCE'S TACOS

RICH AND MEATY SPAGHETTI

MONGOLIAN BEEF

EASY BEEF STROGANOFF

TIN FOIL DINNER

HAWAIIAN HAYSTACKS

CREAMY CHICKEN FETTUCCINE ALFREDO

MEAT LOVER'S LASAGNA

CHICKEN ENCHILADAS AND MEXICAN RICE

NAVAJO TACOS

CHICKEN POT

PIE

During my early years of marriage I ate a lot of store-bought frozen pot pies. Not because I wanted to, but because they were cheap. For many years after I refused to even think of pot pies, but eventually decided this was a great way to use up leftovers and the home-made version tasted nothing like those little frozen yuckies! This could be made in full pie size (double filling) but what fun it is to have your own little individual pie. —Tana

INGREDIENTS

2 cups homemade chicken broth (page 12)

¼ cup cornstarch

Real Salt & pepper to taste

½–¾ cup diced cooked chicken

1 cup mixed veggies

LEFTOVER VERSION

2 cups leftover gravy

½–¾ cup diced cooked chicken (or whatever amount you have)

1 cup leftover vegetables (peas, carrots, corn, green beans, broccoli, or whatever you have)

half pastry recipe from page 224

 INSTRUCTIONS

Prepare filling with new gravy—heat 1½ cup broth until boiling, mix remaining ½ broth and cornstarch together. Slowly whisk into hot broth, and cook until thickened. Or heat leftover gravy, adding a little water (1–2 tablespoons) if needed to achieve a smooth texture. Add chicken and veggies.

Preheat oven to 350 degrees. Prepare half-pastry recipe. Divide dough into six portions. Place plastic wrap on counter top, shape one portion into a small disc shape, dust with a small amount of white rice flour. Roll to form a circle the size of your dish. Use a pizza wheel or cookie cutter to trim edges.

Pick up edge of plastic wrap and flip crust onto your hand and then onto a bake pad or parchment lined baking sheet. Cut decorative vents in the pie crust and top with coarse sea salt. Repeat with the remaining 5 dough portions. Bake for 15–18 minutes until golden brown. Fill individual dishes with hot filling mixture and top with baked pie crusts.

CHICKEN TIKKA MASALA

 INSTRUCTIONS

For chicken tikka, cut chicken into large cubes or slices. Combine all other ingredients and mix well. Add chicken, cover and place in refrigerator. Let marinate for 3–4 hours. Preheat oven to 375 degrees. Remove chicken pieces from marinate and place on a baking sheet. Bake for 30–40 minutes until chicken is cooked through or place chicken pieces on skewers and BBQ until fully cooked.

In a deep skillet, melt butter and sauté onions until lightly browned. Purée crushed tomatoes in a blender. Add tomatoes and all other spices to onions and heat through. Add whipping cream and blend together.

Add cooked chicken to the masala sauce and mix together well. Serve with rice.

For naan, in a large glass bowl, dissolve the yeast and sugar in the warm water. Let proof, about 10 minutes. Using a stand mixture, combine the flours, starches, baking powder, xanthan gum, and salt. Mix well. Add the yogurt, olive oil, and vinegar to the frothy yeast. Add the wet mixture in small amounts to the dry mixture; mix well. Keep mixing until the dough comes together; it will be soft and slightly sticky. Cover the dough with plastic wrap and let sit in a warm place for 1–2 hours.

Melt ½ cube of butter and have ready to brush on finished naan. Dough will still be soft and sticky. Divide into 6–8 equal portions (depending on the size of your skillet and how thick you like it). Place plastic wrap on counter top. Sprinkle a little white rice flour on the plastic wrap and on top of the dough. Roll out one portion, shaping it into either in a teardrop or circle. Heat a cast-iron skillet over high heat until it's almost smoking. Pick up plastic by the edge and flip dough onto your hand and lay it into the skillet. Let it cook on each side for approximately 1 minute or until dough is blistering and turning dark brown. If you are making your naan thicker, cover the skillet with a lid while cooking the second side. Slather with butter and enjoy.

Squeeze a fresh lime. It will only take half a lime to get the tablespoon called for in this recipe and you avoid the nasty preservatives in most bottled juice.

AND NAAN BREAD

I love Indian food. I love the spices and I love the cultured dairy. Chicken Tikka Masala is one of my favorites, and even though I don't have a tandoori oven, this dish still tastes just like what I get at my favorite Indian Restaurant. Restaurants don't serve gluten-free naan, so I decided that I needed to make my own recipe. It's quite easy to make, but plan ahead because the dough needs to sit awhile. Feel free to add garlic, onions, fennel, or anything else for different varieties. You may never want to eat out again! —Tana

INGREDIENTS

CHICKEN TIKKA
2 lb. chicken breast in large cubes or slices
1 cup whole milk yogurt
1 Tbsp. garam masala
1 Tbsp. ground ginger
1 Tbsp. garlic, minced
½ Tbsp. paprika
1 Tbsp. Real Salt
1 Tbsp. lime juice
1–2 Tbsp. fresh grated ginger
¼ cup olive oil

MASALA SAUCE
2 Tbsp. butter
1 cup very finely diced onions
4 tsp. minced garlic
1 tsp. ground ginger
1 Tbsp. garam masala
2 tsp. paprika
½ tsp. turmeric powder

1½ tsp. Real Salt
1 cup crushed tomatoes, puréed
½ cup heavy whipping cream
fresh cilantro for garnish

NAAN BREAD
2 tsp. yeast
2 tsp. sugar
¾ cup warm water
¼ cup brown rice flour
¾ cup white rice flour
¾ cup tapioca starch
⅓ cup arrowroot starch
1 tsp. baking powder
1 tsp. xanthan gum
1 tsp. Real Salt
3 Tbsp. plain yogurt
2 Tbsp. olive oil
1 tsp. apple cider vinegar

TANA'S TIPS
TAKE IT UP A NOTCH

If you are using organic russet potatoes and carrots, you don't even need to bother peeling them. The peels are very nutrient dense.

WITH ROOT VEGETABLES

Pot roast is a delicious, easy-to-make weekend dinner. The best thing about pot roast is that you can make wonderfully easy things from the leftovers. Cooking in a Dutch oven makes it even easier because Dutch ovens self brown. The result is a crisp brown outside and a soft juicy inside, and the meat becomes so tender you can flake it with a fork! You may never go back to cooking a roast any other way. —Tana

INGREDIENTS

3–4 lb. beef roast

2 Tbsp. coconut oil

1 tsp. onion salt

1 tsp. seasoning salt

1 tsp. Real Salt

1 tsp. pepper

4 lb. russet potatoes

2 lb. sweet potatoes or yams

6–8 carrots

1 onion

½ tsp. rosemary

½ tsp. onion salt

½ tsp. seasoning salt

½ tsp. Real Salt

½ tsp. pepper

INSTRUCTIONS

Thaw roast. Preheat oven to 300 degrees. Place roast in a Dutch oven (do not trim fat). It can be an enamel coated Dutch oven or a traditional cast iron Dutch oven, either will work perfectly. Spread the coconut oil on top of the roast and season with 1 teaspoon of the listed salts and pepper. Bake for 2½–3 hours.

Peel and dice russet potatoes, sweet potatoes, and carrots. Cut onion into large pieces. Mix vegetables together and add to Dutch oven with roast. Sprinkle with rosemary, salts, and pepper. Bake for 1+ additional hours until vegetables are soft. Let sit for 10–15 minutes. Remove vegetables.

Using a large fork, flake roast meat and dab in a little of the juices at the bottom of the Dutch oven. Store any leftover meat to make additional meals during the week. Leftover vegetables can be used for pot pies or shepherd's pie.

If you've forgotten to thaw the roast, don't worry—follow the same steps outlined above but bake the roast for 1–2 hours longer before adding the vegetables.

··· HAWAIIAN ···

CHICKEN

Bring a touch of the islands to your table. Hawaiian chicken is a speedy meal to make. I really like the combination of onions and pineapple mixed with chicken and a sweet sauce. Serve it over brown rice and you've got a whole meal. —Tana

INGREDIENTS

4 lb. chicken, cubed

1 onion, diced

½ cup butter

1 (28-oz.) bottle gluten-free ketchup

2 (20-oz.) cans of pineapple chunks

2 cups brown sugar

¼ cup lemon juice

3 Tbsp. gluten-free Worcestershire sauce

¼ cup cornstarch

1 tsp. pepper

 INSTRUCTIONS

In a large skillet or Dutch oven, melt butter. Add onions and sauté. After onions are partially cooked, add chicken and cook through. Drain juice from pineapple and reserve. Set pineapple chunks aside to be added later.

Combine ketchup, lemon juice, pineapple juice, Worcestershire sauce, brown sugar, and cornstarch together. Whisk well. Add to cooked onions and chicken. Add pineapple and pepper. Reduce heat, cover, and let thicken, stirring occasionally. Serve over brown rice.

This recipe can also be made in a crockpot. Combine all ingredients and cook for 3 hours or so on high.

WHITE FISH

Getting a lot of fish in your diet is a great thing, but white fish can be boring if you don't add a crust or sauce. This crust turns plain white fish into an elegant, mouthwatering meal. —Tana

INGREDIENTS

1–2 lb. white fish
½ cup ground nuts
½ cup Parmesan cheese
1 tsp. lemon pepper
1 egg, beaten
1 Tbsp. water
coconut oil for frying

 INSTRUCTIONS

Cut fish into portion sizes. Combine egg and water in a pie plate; whisk well. Chop nuts finely by hand or in a food processor. Combine nuts, cheese, and lemon pepper in a pie plate. Dip fish pieces into egg, and coat on all sides.

Dip coated fish into the nut and cheese mixture. Press into the fish, and coat on all sides. Heat oil in a large skillet. Place fish into skillet and fry until golden brown, turning only once.

Serve over a bed of steamed greens and lemon slices.

CRISPY CRUST

TANA'S TIPS — TAKE IT UP A NOTCH

Use an extra virgin cold extracted olive oil in a dark bottle. It is from the first press and the best quality olive oil. The dark bottle helps prevent oxidation from light.

PIZZA

I love pizza, but gluten-free pizza crusts have been a disappointment to me. They seem to be either tough or soggy. I am so happy with this pizza crust because it has enough body to pick up and eat a slice, but it is still tender and chewy—the best of both worlds. It's hard to believe it's gluten-free. —Tana

INGREDIENTS

1 tsp. sugar

½ cup +3 Tbsp. warm water

1 pkg. yeast

¼ cup brown rice flour

⅓ cup white rice flour

½ cup tapioca starch

½ cup potato starch

2 Tbsp. arrowroot starch

1 tsp. xanthan gum

1 tsp. gelatin

½ tsp. Real Salt

2 Tbsp. buttermilk powder

1 tsp. baking powder

½ tsp. dried basil

½ tsp. dried oregano

3 Tbsp. olive oil

1 egg, beaten

1 tsp. apple cider vinegar

 INSTRUCTIONS

Combine sugar and water, sprinkle yeast on top and mix well. Let sit to proof until mixture becomes frothy.

Preheat oven to 425 degrees. Using a stand mixer, combine all dry ingredients and mix well. Combine oil, egg, and vinegar in a bowl. Pour wet ingredients slowly into dry ingredients while mixing; add yeast mixture and continue mixing until everything is well blended. Dough will be very soft and sticky. Place dough on a lightly greased pizza stone. With greased hands spread dough to ½ an inch from the edges, making it as even as possible. Press dough slightly thicker at the edge to give the crust a rimmed edge.

Let stand in a warm place for 10–15 minutes. Bake for 12–14 minutes. Remove from oven and add sauce, cheese, and toppings as desired. Return to oven and bake an additional 10–15 minutes or so, until cheese is melted and lightly browned.

BRUSSELS SPROUTS

Most people turn up their nose when someone says Brussels sprouts, but roasting them with a little garlic and coconut oil turns them from drab to fab. Roast chicken is my favorite; I love the crispy skin, and the meat is always moist and soft. Prep is very simple for roasting chicken and you can use the leftovers in many other dishes. —Tana

INGREDIENTS

ROASTED CHICKEN
2 whole chickens (skin on)
½ cup coconut oil
seasoning salt & pepper

BRUSSELS SPROUTS
1–2 lb. Brussels sprouts
1 tsp. minced garlic
¼–⅓ cup coconut oil, melted
Real Salt & pepper

 INSTRUCTIONS

For chicken, clean, wash, and pat dry two whole chickens. Make sure to remove any giblets. Put both chickens breast-side up in a large baking pan (not a cookie sheet). Add a generous spoonful of coconut oil to the body cavity of both chickens. Rub remaining coconut oil over the breast side, legs, and wings of both chickens. Sprinkle with seasoning salt and pepper. Hint: Be generous with the seasoning salt. Bake chickens at 350 degrees for 3½–4 hours.

For Brussels sprouts, Preheat oven to 400 degrees. Wash, trim, and split Brussels sprouts, if fresh. If frozen, thaw. Spread Brussels sprouts out on a cookie sheet, drizzle a generous amount of melted coconut oil on top and sprinkle on a little minced garlic; shake the pan to mix and coat completely. Sprinkle on Real Salt and pepper and bake for 30–40 minutes or until light browning and crisp spots occur. Your thoughts about Brussels sprouts may never be the same.

SALMON PATTIES AND TARTAR SAUCE WITH

TANA'S TIPS · TAKE IT UP A NOTCH

Potatoes are one of the produce items that are higher in pesticide residue. Buy organic potatoes, especially if you eat them frequently.

RED ROASTED POTATOES

My mom used to make these delicious salmon patties when I was a child. Of course, what she made wasn't gluten-free, so this is my version of a childhood favorite. Frying in coconut oil adds great flavor, nutrition, and flakiness. The tartar sauce is my addition and is great with any kind of fish. The red potatoes are one of my family's most requested potato dishes. —Tana

INGREDIENTS

SALMON PATTIES
2 (7.5-oz.) cans salmon

2 eggs

¾ cup crushed gluten-free crackers or gluten-free bread crumbs

1 tsp. lemon juice

½ tsp. lemon pepper

¼ tsp. salt

⅛ tsp. black pepper

HOMEMADE TARTAR SAUCE
1 cup mayonnaise

¼ cup minced dill pickles

1 Tbsp. dry minced onion

1 Tbsp. lemon juice

1 Tbsp. pickle juice

½ tsp. Real Salt

1 tsp. lemon pepper

½ tsp. minced dill

ROASTED RED POTATOES
4 lb. red potatoes

⅓ cup coconut oil

2 tsp. minced garlic

1 Tbsp. dried parsley

2 tsp. Real Salt

1 tsp. pepper

 INSTRUCTIONS

Drain juice from salmon (remove bones and skin if salmon is not boneless skinless) and break apart with a fork. Mix in remaining ingredients. Form patties and fry in coconut oil until browned.

Hydrate dried onion with lemon and pickle juice. Add all other ingredients and mix well.

Preheat oven to 350 degrees. Wash potatoes and cut in quarters. Melt coconut oil in a 9 × 13 baking pan (it melts very quickly). Carefully remove from oven and add potatoes and remaining ingredients. Stir to coat and evenly disperse coconut oil and spices. Bake for 45–60 minutes uncovered.

SHEPHERD'S

PIE

This old world pub meal has become an American favorite. Sitting down to a hearty plate of ground beef, mashed potatoes, veggies, and a thick gravy, all wrapped up in a flaky, delicious pie crust will please your entire crowd. Shepherd's Pie is my standby for using up all those leftovers, especially mashed potatoes, and you can really include any vegetables you have—it doesn't have to be the standard fare. The entire meal can be made from leftovers! —Tana

INGREDIENTS

½ pastry crust recipe (page 224)

1–2 lb. ground beef, cooked (leftover)

4–6 cups mashed potatoes (leftover) or cook and mash 4 large potatoes

1–1½ cups leftover veggies of your choice, or 10 oz. frozen mixed veggies, thawed + 1 Tbsp. dried minced onion

3–4 cups leftover gravy

4–6 slices cheddar cheese

INSTRUCTIONS

Make a single pastry crust. Preheat oven to 400 degrees. If you make a new gravy for this dish, heat 3 cups of your home-made beef broth. Add salt and pepper to taste. Mix 1 cup beef broth and ½ cup cornstarch together and add to hot broth. Continue heating, whisking occasionally until broth thickens.

Combine ground beef, veggies, and gravy. Spoon into an unbaked pie shell. Spread mashed potatoes over the top of the beef mixture and cover with cheese.

Bake for 25–30 minutes if ingredients are warm. If using all cold leftovers bake for 35+ minutes.

SWEET & SOUR CHICKEN

WITH HAM FRIED RICE

It is nearly impossible to get this dish gluten-free when you are eating out, but we shouldn't have to miss out on it; just make it yourself at home. You'll get a larger portion and save a little money too. —Tana

INGREDIENTS

3 lb. chicken, cut into bite-size cubes

coconut oil

BATTER

¼ cup brown rice flour

¼ cup white rice flour

¼ cup sorghum flour

½ cup tapioca starch

½ cup potato starch

1 tsp. baking powder

1 Tbsp. arrowroot starch

½ tsp. xanthan gum

2 tsp. Real Salt

½ tsp. turmeric

2 tsp. olive oil

1¼ cups water

SAUCE

1 (20-oz.) can pineapple tidbits in juice

4 Tbsp. gluten-free ketchup

½ cup apple cider vinegar

1½ cups brown sugar

5 Tbsp. cornstarch

HAM FRIED RICE

4 cups cooked brown rice

6 oz. ham, diced

4–5 green onions, sliced

1 cup frozen peas, thawed

3 eggs, beaten

¼–⅓ cup gluten-free tamari soy sauce

2 Tbsp. coconut oil

 INSTRUCTIONS

For chicken, heat coconut oil to 315–350 degrees in a deep fryer or a small diameter pot. The oil needs to be 3–4 inches deep. Combine all dry ingredients and mix well. Add olive oil and water and whisk together with dry ingredients until smooth and well blended. Dip chicken into batter to coat, and fry in hot coconut oil until lightly browned.

For sauce, drain juice from pineapple. Combine pineapple juice and enough water to equal 2 cups of liquid. Combine liquid, vinegar, and ketchup together and start heating in a medium saucepan. Mix brown sugar and cornstarch together and add into liquid before it gets very warm. Cook sauce, whisking occasionally, until it appears clear instead of cloudy and has thickened. Fold in pineapple tidbits (if desired). Serve over battered chicken.

In a skillet, heat 1 tablespoon coconut oil. Fry eggs, mixing until well scrambled. Remove from skillet. Add 1 tablespoon coconut oil and lightly fry diced ham and onions. Add in rice, peas, and scrambled eggs. Pour soy sauce over the mixture and mix well. Heat through. Serve as a side to Sweet & Sour Chicken.

Nº 110 SWEET & SPICY

···PORK ROAST···

This has quickly become my favorite way of making pork roast. It is lightly sweet with a little zip and it is easy, easy, easy! Any leftover is great reheated the next day by itself or wrapped in a tortilla with a little cheese and veggies. —Tana

INGREDIENTS

3 lb. pork roast (loin or shoulder), thawed

1 (20-oz.) can crushed pineapple

1 (16-oz.) jar sliced pepperoncinis

 INSTRUCTIONS

Place roast in a crockpot. Cover with crushed pineapple and pepperoncinis. Set on low for 8–10 hours. When ready to serve, use a large fork to flake roast into juice and mix together. I almost feel bad there is not more to this recipe, but why feel bad for something that is so easy and is amazingly delicious!

CROCKPOT RIBS &

TANA'S TIPS
TAKE IT UP A NOTCH

It's a good idea to buy organic potatoes when you intend to eat the peel.

TWICE-BAKED POTATOES

Making ribs can often times be very time consuming and labor intensive. This recipe makes mouthwatering, tender ribs without all the time and hassle. My father-in-law, the family rib connoisseur, gave them a big approval, which was validation for me that we got the recipe right. —Chandice

INGREDIENTS

1–2 lb. baby back ribs

½ tsp. ground ginger

½ tsp. cumin

¼ tsp. cayenne

1 Tbsp. smoked paprika (regular paprika is fine as well)

1 tsp. Real Salt

1 tsp. black pepper

1 Tbsp. brown sugar

BBQ Sauce (see p. 208)

TWICE-BAKED POTATOES

4 large russet potatoes

3 Tbsp. butter

¼ cup sour cream

¼ cup milk

1 tsp. Real Salt

½ tsp. black pepper

8 slices cheddar cheese

 INSTRUCTIONS

Combine all the ingredients except the meat and BBQ sauce. Massage spice mixture into all areas of the meat. Cut one piece of ribs large enough to cover the bottom of the Crockpot (about 4 riblets). Cut the remaining ribs into individual pieces and stand up, placing meaty side against edge of Crockpot. It will resemble a crown of ribs. Every piece of meat should touch some surface of the Crockpot. Cook on low 6 hours or until the ribs are tender. Remove and place on a baking sheet. Baste with gluten-free BBQ sauce of your choosing and broil for 1–2 minutes.

For the twice-baked potatoes, preheat the oven to 400 degrees. Thoroughly wash russet potatoes and then poke with a fork in multiple places. Cook potatoes for 1 hour or until tender when poked with a fork. Using a hot pad or towel, remove potatoes from oven. Slice in half lengthwise. Using a spoon, scoop out potato centers, making sure to leave enough so that existing shells don't break in half. Add butter to hot potato centers removed from shells and combine well until melted. Add in sour cream, milk, salt, and pepper. Whip until the consistency of mashed potatoes. Spoon mashed potato mixture into each shell and top with a slice of cheddar cheese. Broil for 3 minutes or until cheese is melted.

INSIDE-OUT BURGERS AND HOMEMADE POTATO CHIPS

These burgers are juicy and filled with flavor. That first bite where melted cheese oozes out will make even the most seasoned burger lover a huge fan of this recipe. Pair it with homemade potato chips cooked in coconut oil and you have a summer meal made in Heaven. —Chandice

INGREDIENTS

1 lb. ground beef
½ onion, diced
⅓ cup shredded cheddar cheese

FOR THE CHIPS
3 peeled potatoes, sliced very thin
coconut oil for frying
½ tsp. Real Salt
½ tsp. black pepper

 INSTRUCTIONS

For the burgers, fry onions until they just begin to soften. Split the beef into four equal parts and form two parts into little dishes leaving a canyon with straight sides in the center. Place onions in both dishes and top each with half the cheese. If you like grilled onions, grill them before adding to the meat. Take the remaining two parts of hamburger and place over dishes sealing the edges and flattening just a little bit. Grill patties until they are done to your liking.

For the chips, heat coconut oil in your deep fryer or saucepan until hot enough that when a sprinkle of water is dropped in, it sizzles. Fry potato chips in small batches until crisp. Drain on paper towels and sprinkle with salt and pepper.

TANA'S TIPS TAKE IT UP A NOTCH

Use a high quality organic grass-fed ground beef; it is so juicy and flavorful.

THREE-CHEESE
WHITE SAUCE LASAGNA

White sauce and chicken lasagna is a marvelous change from regular lasagna. My son says it's the best lasagna he's ever had. I love all the extra cheese of this dish, and since it reheats so well, making a big pan and having leftovers makes the whole family happy. —Tana

#115

INGREDIENTS

½ cup butter

2 cups cream

2 tsp. minced garlic

2 tsp. oregano

1 tsp. basil

½ tsp. Real Salt

½ tsp. pepper

2¼ cups Parmesan cheese

15 oz. ricotta or cottage cheese

8 oz. mozzarella cheese, grated

6 cups lightly packed fresh spinach, or 2 (10-oz.) pkg. frozen spinach, thawed and drained

8–12 lasagna noodles

INSTRUCTIONS

Preheat oven to 350 degrees. Cook lasagna noodles according to the manufacturer's directions minus a minute or two so the noodles are a little al dente. Rinse with cold water.

In a large sauce pan, melt butter. Add cream, spices, and 2 cups of Parmesan cheese. When warm, add spinach to pan, cover, and let cook for 2–3 minutes until spinach softens. Remove from heat. Fold in the ricotta or cottage cheese.

Place ⅓ of the sauce in the bottom of a 9 × 13 pan. Layer 3–4 noodles on top of the sauce, add another layer of sauce, one more layer of noodles, and a final layer of sauce. Top with mozzarella cheese and sprinkle the remaining ¼ cup of Parmesan cheese on the top. Bake uncovered for 35–45 minutes.

TANA'S TIPS • TAKE IT UP A NOTCH

Use fresh basil and oregano for an added flavor punch!

CREAMY ITALIAN CHICKEN

This is my favorite dinner that my mama Sheila used to make for me. It was one of the first that I knew I wanted to convert to gluten-free after my celiac diagnosis. This chicken recipe is so creamy and flavorful. Sheila would always make it when I came to visit because she knew how much I loved it. You guys are going to love it too! —Chandice

INGREDIENTS

2 lb. chicken thighs or breasts

½ Tbsp. garlic

1 tsp. sugar

½ Tbsp. onion powder

1 Tbsp. dried oregano

½ tsp. black pepper

¼ tsp. dried thyme

½ tsp. dried basil

½ tsp. dried parsley

¼ tsp. celery salt

1 Tbsp. Real Salt

2 (8-oz.) pkgs. cream cheese

2 cups homemade cream of chicken soup (page 80)

Real Salt and pepper to taste

 INSTRUCTIONS

Put all the ingredients in a crockpot and cook on low 6–8 hrs. Chicken will be pull-apart tender. Serve hot over rice. We always enjoyed it with corn and cottage cheese as well.

TACO CASSEROLE

This casserole is so delicious, with all the traditional flavors of your favorite taco without the mess. It is great for using all your taco leftovers from another night as it marries the flavors to create another great dish that kids and grown ups alike will fall in love with it. —Chandice

INGREDIENTS

1 lb. ground beef, or the equivalent in leftover cooked ground beef

2 cups frozen corn

9–12 gluten-free corn tortillas

1 cup black olives, sliced

2 cups shredded cheddar cheese

1 (15-oz.) can tomato sauce

1 tsp. cornstarch

1 Tbsp. chili powder

1 tsp. cumin

½ tsp. Real Garlic Salt

½ tsp. Real Onion Salt

½ tsp. black pepper

1 tsp. oregano

 INSTRUCTIONS

Preheat oven to 350 degrees. If not using leftovers, fry the beef until cooked all the way through, making sure to break in to small bite size pieces.

In a saucepan, combine the tomato sauce, cornstarch, chili powder, cumin, oregano, salts, and pepper and bring to a boil. Spread a little at the bottom of a round, or 8 × 8 baking dish.

Layer the casserole in this order: tortillas (dipped in enchilada sauce until completely covered), beef, corn, olives, and cheese. Repeat ending with cheese on top. Bake, covered with tin foil, for 25–35 minutes or until hot all the way through. Remove the tin foil and broil for 3–5 minutes. Top with gluten-free ranch dressing or sour cream and fresh cilantro.

GRANDMA JOYCE'S TACOS

Growing up, my mom and siblings had tacos almost every single night the winter after her mom passed away. It was one of the only things the kids knew how to make. Each of them carried their love for tacos into their future families by doing taco night weekly. Now my boys love tacos because I do them often, just like Grandma Joyce used to do for my mom. —Chandice

INGREDIENTS

1 lb. ground beef

1 Tbsp. cumin

1 tsp. chili powder

1 tsp. Real Onion Salt

1 tsp. Real Garlic Salt

1 tsp. black pepper

¼ cup water

¼ cup finely chopped onion

corn tortillas

butter as needed for tortillas

taco toppings: diced tomatoes, lettuce, cheese, olives, salsa

 INSTRUCTIONS

In a frying pan, brown the meat until the pink is almost gone. Be sure to break into smaller pieces while cooking. Add the water, seasonings, and onion. Continue cooking until the meat gets a little bit crispy on the edges. Transfer meat to a bowl and top with aluminum foil to keep warm.

Spread butter on both sides of two corn tortillas, or three tortillas if you have a large frying pan, and cook on each side about a minute or until they have nice color but aren't crispy. Repeat until all of the shells are cooked. Make sure to keep them in a tortilla warmer or on a plate covered with aluminum foil so they don't get cold before serving.

TANA'S
TIPS
TAKE IT UP A NOTCH

Buy non-GMO corn tortillas with a short ingredient list (ie: corn, water, lime, salt). Avoid tortillas with colorings, parabens, and preservatives.

RICH AND MEATY SPAGHETTI

This is another recipe from Debbie Probst that she has been cooking for her family for over 30 years. When I married my husband, he let me know that this was his favorite dish his mom made and that he would love if I learned how to make it as well. Thank goodness it is easy so that I didn't feel overwhelmed in trying. While I think my recipe has finally reached the level of my mother-in-law's, my husband still has a soft spot for his mom's. —Chandice

INGREDIENTS

2 lb. hamburger

1 (46-oz.) can tomato juice

1 (8-oz.) can tomato sauce

1 Tbsp. chili powder

1 Tbsp. oregano

1 Tbsp. parsley

1 onion

1 pkg. brown rice pasta

 INSTRUCTIONS

Brown the hamburger and onion, and then sprinkle with cornstarch. Stir in tomato juice, tomato sauce, chili powder, oregano, and parsley. To get the best flavor, simmer for 5 hours over low heat, stirring often. Serve hot over prepared brown rice pasta.

···• MONGOLIAN •···

BEEF

Restaurant Mongolian beef is one of the tastiest dishes but can often be pricey and is rarely gluten-free. I decided to create this dish to satisfy my craving. I hope it satisfies yours as well. My husband requested I start making it weekly, so that is a good sign, especially since he does not have to live gluten-free and is my toughest critic. Love you, hun! —Chandice

INGREDIENTS

SAUCE

2 tsp. coconut oil

1 tsp. ginger, minced

2 tsp. minced garlic

½ cup gluten-free soy sauce

½ cup water

¼ cup honey

¼ cup brown sugar

MEAT

⅓ cup coconut oil

1 lb. steak, any cut, thinly sliced

¼ cup cornstarch

1 tsp. Real Salt

1 tsp. cayenne

1 cup sliced green onions, in 2-inch segments

 INSTRUCTIONS

For sauce, combine oil, garlic, and ginger over medium heat. Cook about 2 minutes. Add the gluten-free soy sauce, water, and honey. Boil until mixture starts to thicken (about 5 minutes).

Combine cornstarch, salt, and cayenne in a bowl. Sprinkle the meat with that mixture and let sit for 5 minutes so that the cornstarch sticks. Heat frying oil in a large skillet and cook meat in the hot oil until medium rare. Add the sauce and cook meat until it is done to your liking.

TANA'S **TIPS** TAKE IT UP A NOTCH

Buy an organic, grass-fed cut of beef.

This meal is a great way to use your leftover ground beef from another dinner. The sauce is so rich and full of flavor that it brings a whole new depth of flavor to the leftover meat. We also choose to use our leftover chicken broth seasoned with gluten-free Worcestershire so we can save money and not have to buy beef broth. If you have leftover beef broth from a roast, this would be a great place to use it. Feel free to serve this over rice or gluten-free noodles; however, I personally recommend noodles. —Chandice

INGREDIENTS

1 lb. ground beef

1 pint sour cream

2 cups homemade chicken broth (p. 12)

1 Tbsp. gluten-free Worcestershire sauce

1 Tbsp. dried parsley

1 tsp. Real Salt

½ tsp. black pepper

rice or gluten-free egg noodles

INSTRUCTIONS

Crumble and cook or reheat your ground beef. Add the remaining ingredients except for rice or egg noodles and cook on medium heat until hot. Serve over prepared rice or egg noodles.

TIN FOIL DINNER

There couldn't be an easier meal than tin foil dinners. They take 5–10 minutes to prepare and taste fantastic after being cooked over an open fire. When we are craving these at home, I just bake them in the oven. They are great no matter which way you choose to cook them. —Chandice

INGREDIENTS

1 lb. ground beef

1 small bag baby carrots

2 medium potatoes

1 medium onion

Real Salt and pepper

 INSTRUCTIONS

Lay out four rectangle pieces of tin foil that are roughly one foot long each. Lay another the same size over each. Divide the beef into four parts and flatten into patties. Place the patties on the center of the tin foil and season with a little salt and pepper.

After washing your hands, slice the potatoes into thin slices and layer evenly over the patties. Sprinkle the baby carrots over the potatoes and around the meat patties evenly. Gather the long ends of the tin foil and lay one over the other making sure to bring in the sides as well then seal all edges. Bake at 350 degrees for 45–60 minutes or until potatoes are softened.

If cooking over an open fire, place directly on a small pile of hot coals and cook 10–15 minutes, turning over half way through. Check meat and potatoes and cook longer if needed; depending on how hot your coals are, you may need a longer cook time.

This is a fantastic meal for using all your leftover vegetables as well as leftover chicken and chicken broth. It is amazing how using all of these leftovers in this unique way can create a tasty new dish that the whole family will love. —Chandice

INGREDIENTS

4 cups homemade chicken broth (page 12)

½ cup cornstarch

1 tsp. Real Salt

1 tsp. black pepper

2 cups leftover shredded chicken

toppings: olives, shredded coconut, green onions, pineapple, carrots, green pepper, and shredded cheese

rice for serving

 INSTRUCTIONS

In a medium saucepan, heat 3 cups of the chicken broth to a boil. In a bowl, whisk together the unheated cup of broth and cornstarch. Slowly whisk it into the hot broth and continue whisking as you add the salt and pepper. Stir in the shredded chicken. Meanwhile, cook some rice in a rice cooker so you have it for serving the sauce over. Cut the toppings. Enjoy hot over cooked rice with your choice of toppings.

TANA'S • TAKE IT UP A NOTCH • TIPS

This wonderful meal incorporates a lot of fresh veggies, so buy as much organic as possible.

CREAMY CHICKEN FETTUCCINE ALFREDO

I think this is a dish that nearly everyone loves. I haven't met a person who isn't smitten with a good fettuccine alfredo. There are many great recipes but ours has the secret to making the best fettuccine around . . . ground nutmeg. Would you believe it? This sweet spice gives the creamy sauce an amazing taste that you won't soon forget. —Chandice

INGREDIENTS

1 cup Parmesan cheese

1 cup whipping cream

1 stick butter

1 tsp. minced garlic

1 tsp. nutmeg

dash of black pepper

2 cups leftover shredded chicken

1 (16-oz.) bag gluten-free fettuccine pasta

 INSTRUCTIONS

In a large stockpot, prepare the gluten-free noodles as directed on the package.

Meanwhile, in a medium saucepan, melt the butter. Whisk in the whipped cream, garlic, nutmeg, and pepper. Once a light boil begins, whisk in the Parmesan and remove from heat. Stir in the chicken. Pour over drained noodles and toss to coat. Serve hot with more fresh nutmeg.

TANA'S TIPS TAKE IT UP A NOTCH

Nutmeg is the secret ingredient in this dish that makes it amazing. Use fresh ground nutmeg and really take it over the top.

MEAT LOVER'S

··· LASAGNA ···

Lasagna is a dish that most love. This recipe takes a classic favorite to the next level by using half beef and half sausage, which gives it a spicy, notable flavor that can often be missed when only using beef. Because of all the great spices and rich tomato sauce used, this recipe is definitely one I recommend using your leftover ground beef in. —Chandice

INGREDIENTS

1 lb. ground beef

1 lb. ground gluten-free sausage

8 oz. mozzarella cheese, grated

1 cup Parmesan cheese

16 oz. cottage cheese

2 boxes gluten-free lasagna noodles

2 (15-oz.) cans tomato sauce

1 small onion, diced

1 tsp. coconut oil

1 tsp. dried basil

1 tsp. dried oregano

1 tsp. minced garlic

1 tsp. Real Salt

 INSTRUCTIONS

Preheat the oven to 350 degrees. In a frying pan, crumble and fry the meat. In a saucepan, heat the coconut oil until hot but not smoking. Add the onion and cook until begins to soften and turns golden.

Add the tomato sauce and spices. Spread a little sauce on the bottom of a 9 × 13 pan and top with 3–4 noodles. Top with more sauce, cottage cheese, meat, Parmesan, and mozzarella. Continue layering this way until there is about a half an inch remaining at the top of the pan. Cover with tin foil and bake at 350 degrees for 35 minutes. Remove the tin foil and bake another 10–15 minutes. Noodles should be softened and cheese bubbling.

TANA'S TIPS TAKE IT UP A NOTCH

Did you know that cheese isn't naturally orange? Use a natural organic cheese and avoid any added coloring.

MEXICAN RICE

We love making this anytime because it is so simple and turns out so full of flavor. This is a great recipe to use your leftover shredded chicken in. After living in Arizona for 8 years, Mexican food became part of our weekly meal plans. We can't do without at least one Mexican dinner a week now. —Chandice

INGREDIENTS

1 Tbsp. brown rice flour

1 Tbsp. cornstarch

2 Tbsp. coconut or olive oil

1 Tbsp. chili powder

1 tsp. cumin

1 tsp. salt

½ tsp. garlic powder

2 cups tomato sauce

1 cup water

8 corn tortillas

2 cups shredded chicken (leftovers from roasted chicken work great)

1 (4-oz.) can diced green chilies

1 cup sour cream

½ tsp. salt

¼ tsp. black pepper

2½ cups shredded cheddar cheese

MEXICAN RICE

1½ cups raw brown rice

2 cups homemade chicken broth (p 12)

1 (15-oz.) can diced tomatoes, undrained

1 tsp. Cholula or other hot sauce

1 tsp. Real Salt

1 tsp. minced garlic

1 tsp. cumin

INSTRUCTIONS

Combine the first nine ingredients in a saucepan and whisk together well. Heat over medium heat until it begins to boil and thicken. Preheat the oven to 350 degrees. In another bowl, combine the chicken, sour cream, green chilies, and salt and pepper, along with 1¼ cups shredded cheese.

In a 9 × 13 glass baking dish, spread half a cup of the prepared enchilada sauce over the bottom of the pan. Spread 2–3 Tbsp. of chicken mixture in one tortilla at a time then roll and place seems side down in the baking dish being careful not to break the tortillas. Once all have been placed in the dish, spread with the remaining sauce and sprinkle with the remaining cheese. Bake at 350 degrees for 45 minutes.

For the rice, combine all ingredients in your rice cooker and cook until the machine lets you know it is done. If you don't have a rice cooker, prepare the rice by combining all the ingredients and bring to a boil. Reduce heat to low, cover and simmer for 25–30, or until the rice is soft. Fluff with a fork and serve hot.

TACOS

Navajo tacos are yummy fry bread or fried scones topped with chili and/or other taco ingredients. You might find them at your local fair, but they certainly won't be gluten-free. Now you don't have to miss out on them; just make them yourself at home. —Tana

INGREDIENTS

1¼ cups white rice flour

¼ cup brown rice flour

¼ cup sorghum flour

½ cup tapioca starch

¾ cup potato starch

1 tsp. xanthan gum

1 Tbsp. baking powder

1 tsp. Real Salt

1 Tbsp. coconut oil, melted, plus more for frying

2 eggs, beaten

½ cup warm water

¼ cup warm buttermilk

1 tsp. apple cider vinegar

 ## INSTRUCTIONS

Combine all dry ingredients. Mix in all wet ingredients and blend well. Let dough sit for 10–15 minutes. Heat coconut oil in a deep skillet. Divide dough into 10 pieces.

You can either shape the dough with greased hands or lay out a piece of plastic wrap, dust lightly with rice flour. Shape dough into a disc shape and roll out into a circle. Place dough in hot oil and cook on each side until golden brown. Drain oil on a paper towel.

Serve with chili on page 82, topped with cheese, lettuce, tomatoes, green onions, and black olives.

TANA'S
TIPS
TAKE IT UP A NOTCH

Coconut oil is my favorite frying oil. It withstands a fairly high heat and produces a crisp golden crust.

👉 bread & rolls

MINI BANANA BREAD LOAVES

BUTTERMILK BISCUITS

CHEESY CHIVE BISCUITS

CHEESY JALAPEÑO CORNBREAD

CRAZY GOOD POTATO ROLLS

HEARTY OAT BREAD

HONEY SWEET CORNBREAD

PÃO DE QUEIJO

MINI BANANA BREAD

LOAVES

Who doesn't love soft, moist banana bread? Banana bread is already dark so adding some nutritious teff flour is a great boost. Mini loaves are great way to change up the old stand-by, providing a nice addition to each plate without the fuss or mess of cutting individual slices. Banana bread works well with breakfast, dinner, or as a snack and it's definitely one of the best ways to use up those over-ripe bananas. —Tana

INGREDIENTS

⅓ cup almond flour

⅓ cup teff flour

¼ cup sorghum flour

3 Tbsp. brown rice flour

½ cup tapioca starch

¼ cup potato starch

2 Tbsp. coconut flour

1 tsp. xanthan gum

1 tsp. baking power

½ tsp. Real Salt

½ cup butter

1 cup brown sugar

2 eggs

1 tsp. gluten-free vanilla

1 Tbsp. lemon juice

2 ripe bananas, mashed

½ cup chopped walnuts (optional)

 INSTRUCTIONS

Preheat oven to 350 degrees. In a stand mixer, cream butter and sugar together. Add eggs and mix well. Add in vanilla, lemon juice and mashed bananas. Combine together all dry ingredients. Add a cup at a time to wet mixture.

Mix until blended, but do not over mix. Pour into greased mini loaf pans and bake for 20–22 minutes (toothpick in center will come out clean).

TANA'S
TIPS
TAKE IT UP A NOTCH

Teff is a highly nutritious gluten-free grain, higher in protein, fiber, calcium, potassium, and iron than most other grains. Don't be afraid to increase the teff even further by reducing the tapioca starch by ⅛ cup to ¼ cup and replacing it with an extra ⅛ to ¼ cup of teff. This will make your bread slightly heavier, but still really tasty, and the nutritional benefit of the extra teff is worth it.

BUTTERMILK

BISCUITS

As Agnes from Despicable Me would say, "It's so fluffy I'm gonna die!" Who would have thought you could get a gluten-free buttermilk biscuit that is as good as the original thing. It can be tough to make a gluten-free version that is flaky and fluffy, but cultured dairy lightens and apple cider vinegar helps with flakiness. Arrowroot and gelatin are important in this recipe because they act as binders when not using any eggs. Top these light fluffy biscuits with butter, honey, or jam. Enjoy! —Tana

INGREDIENTS

⅓ cup brown rice flour

⅓ cup sorghum flour

½ cup tapioca starch

½ cup potato starch

2 Tbsp. almond flour

2 Tbsp. arrowroot

1 Tbsp. coconut flour

4 tsp. baking powder

1 tsp. gelatin

1 tsp. xanthan gum

1 tsp. Real Salt

⅔ cup butter, cold

½ cup buttermilk

½ cup sour cream

1 tsp. apple cider vinegar

INSTRUCTIONS

In a stand mixer, combine all dry ingredients. Using a cheese grater on large or coarse size, grate butter into flours and mix until crumbly. Stir in buttermilk, sour cream, and vinegar. Heat oven to 450 degrees. Let mixture rest for 20–25 minutes.

Working with small portions, shape dough with hands on parchment or a non-stick baking sheet, to 1 inch thick, and cut into rounds with a cookie cutter. Repeat with remaining dough for 8 biscuits. Bake on a parchment or non-stick covered cook sheet for 13–15 minutes or until lightly browned.

TANA'S TIPS TAKE IT UP A NOTCH

Use aluminum-free baking powder. There are several brands on the market, so it should not be difficult to find one and it will only cost you a few cents more to make this important change. Note: Baking soda does not contain aluminum.

CHEESY CHIVE

···BISCUITS···

These biscuits are very similar to ones served at a popular restaurant chain. When they brought out those warm cheesy biscuits I felt like it was the best part of the meal. Why live without something I enjoy so much? Well, I don't have to, because I've created my own gluten-free version. Now I'm not missing a thing.
—Tana

INGREDIENTS

⅓ cup brown rice flour	1 Tbsp. dried chives
⅓ cup sorghum flour	½ tsp. dill
½ cup tapioca starch	1 tsp. minced garlic
½ cup potato starch	⅓ cup butter, cold
2 Tbsp. almond flour	1 egg, beaten
2 Tbsp. arrowroot	¾ cup buttermilk
1 Tbsp. coconut flour	1 tsp. apple cider vinegar
4 tsp. baking powder	1 cup grated cheese
1 tsp. gelatin	2–4 Tbsp. butter, melted
1 tsp. xanthan gum	Parmesan cheese
1 tsp. Real Salt	

 INSTRUCTIONS

Using a stand mixer, combine all dry flours and spices. Using a cheese grater on large or coarse size, grate butter into flours and mix until crumbly. Stir in garlic, egg, buttermilk, and vinegar until blended. Mix in grated cheese. Heat oven to 450 degrees. Let mixture rest for 20–25 minutes.

Drop dough with large spoon onto parchment or a non-stick baking sheet. Bake for 13–15 minutes, or until lightly browned. Remove from oven and brush with butter, sprinkle with Parmesan cheese. Makes 8 large or 16 small biscuits.

TANA'S **TIPS** TAKE IT UP A NOTCH

Not all salt is "real"; most conventional salt is highly processed. This processing removes most all the natural minerals. Salt is essential to your health, so make sure to choose one that improves it. I love Real Salt!

CHEESY JALAPEÑO

№ 140

CORNBREAD

For those who like a more savory and spicy style of cornbread, here is a great gluten-free version for you. Two types of cheese make it very cheesy and jalapeños give it just the right kick. It's great paired with chili, spicy soup, or any south-of-the-border meal. —Tana

#141

INGREDIENTS

⅓ cup almond flour	2 tsp. Real Salt
¼ cup brown rice flour	⅓ cup frozen, fresh, or canned corn, drained
¼ cup sorghum flour	½ jalapeño pepper, minced
2 Tbsp. teff flour	2 Tbsp. honey
⅓ cup tapioca starch	¼ cup butter
¼ cup cornstarch	2 eggs, beaten
1 tsp. xanthan gum	¼ cup sour cream
1 cup finely ground cornmeal	1 cup buttermilk
1 tsp. baking powder	1 cup grated cheddar cheese
1 tsp. baking soda	1 cup grated pepper jack cheese

 INSTRUCTIONS

Thaw corn kernels. Using a stand mixer, combine the dry ingredients; mix well. Melt butter and cool. Dice corn kernels and mince jalapeño pepper (use gloves to protect your hands, and avoid touching your face). Add honey, eggs, sour cream, and buttermilk to melted butter; mix. Stir into dry ingredients until blended. Let stand for 15 minutes.

Preheat oven to 400 degrees. Fold in cheese. Pour into a 10"square or round greased pan. Bake for 20–25 minutes or until a toothpick inserted in center comes out clean.

TANA'S **TIPS** TAKE IT UP A NOTCH

Use non-GMO cornmeal and cornstarch. Most of the corn produced in the U.S. is GMO; look specifically for one labeled non-GMO. It is not as important that corn products be organic because they are actually low in pesticide residue.

TANA'S TIPS · TAKE IT UP A NOTCH

Try using sprouted brown rice flour; it really improves the texture and lightens up any bread recipe.

POTATO ROLLS

Bread and pies have always been my forte. So coming up with an amazing gluten-free roll recipe was at the top of my list (and the top of the request list for my non-gluten-free family). They need to have a light texture that separates in layers when you pull them apart, and of course the flavor has to be like regular bread, nothing weird. They also have to be amazing right from the oven, but still good cold for leftover turkey sandwiches and reheat really great if you just want a plain roll and butter. Most of the time these don't last long enough to eat as leftover, but when I make a big batch and they do, I know they will not go to waste. —Tana

#143

INGREDIENTS

1 Tbsp. milled chia seeds, soaked in ¼ cup warm water

1 Tbsp. yeast

1 cup brown rice flour

½ cup white rice flour

1 cup potato starch

1 cup tapioca starch

½ cup sorghum flour

½ cup almond flour

3 tsp. xanthan gum

2 tsp. baking powder

1½ tsp. Real Salt

½ cup mashed potatoes (use leftover)

1 cup warm milk

1 Tbsp. sugar

½ cup coconut oil, melted and cooled

½ cup butter, soft or melted

2 eggs

½ cup honey

2 tsp. buttermilk powder

1 tsp. apple cider vinegar

 INSTRUCTIONS

Put 1 tablespoon milled chia seed in a ¼ measuring cup, fill with warm water, and it let soak. Dissolve yeast and sugar in warm milk. Let sit to proof. This recipe will work best using a stand mixer with the paddle. Combine all flours, starches, xanthan gum, and baking powder.

Mix the mashed potatoes, honey coconut oil, butter, eggs, and chia seeds together. Add the yeast mixture and start adding the dry ingredients slowly while mixing until well blended and smooth. Dough will be sticky. Grease a 9 × 13 pan lightly with coconut oil.

Using a ½ cup ice cream scoop, scoop dough and place in greased hands. Roll dough into a ball and place into baking pan. Cover and place in a warm place for 1–2 hours until dough is nearly doubled in size. If you would like the tops to brown a little better, brush lightly with a beaten egg. Bake at 350 degrees for 20–22 minutes. Brush tops with melted butter.

··· OAT BREAD ···

My husband loves bread. His mother used to make homemade whole wheat bread a couple times a week. I think he had more anxiety over my gluten-free diet than I did because I stopped making him bread. It was like a hole in his heart, or should I say his stomach. He has been so excited for all the great gluten-free bread recipes I've created. He especially likes this one because it reminds him of better (bread) days!—Tana

INGREDIENTS

2 Tbsp. milled chia seeds

⅓ cup warm water

¼ cup sugar

3 Tbsp. yeast

1 cup warm water

2 cups gluten-free oat flour

1½ cups white rice flour

⅓ cup brown rice flour

¼ cup sorghum flour

1 cup potato starch

¾ cup tapioca starch

⅛ cup coconut flour

1 tsp. xanthan gum

1 tsp. Real Salt

2 tsp. baking powder

2 Tbsp. buttermilk powder

2 Tbsp. psyllium husk powder

4 eggs, beaten

½ cup butter, melted

1 cup lukewarm milk

¼ cup honey

1 Tbsp. apple cider vinegar

 INSTRUCTIONS

Combine ⅓ cup warm water and milled chia; let soak. In another bowl combine sugar, yeast, and 1 cup warm water; let proof. Using a stand mixer with a paddle, mix together all dry ingredients from oat flour to psyllium husk. Make a well in the center of the dry ingredients and add the eggs, milk, honey, and vinegar. Start mixing together, add in the chia seed and yeast mixture, and continue mixing, scraping down bowl as needed, until all ingredients are well combined. Beat for an additional 3–4 minutes at a medium speed. Dough will be thick, but still a little sticky. Let dough rest for 30 minutes.

Grease a loaf pan with coconut oil. Transfer dough into the loaf pan, shaping dough with a spatula and smoothing at edges. Place dough in a warm place or in the oven on bread proof setting for 1–2 hours until dough has nearly doubled in size. Heat oven to 350 degrees. Brush loaf top with a beaten egg, sprinkle with additional oats and coarse sea salt. Bake for 60–70 minutes. Cool bread on a wire rack for 10 minutes or so before removing from pan.

HONEY SWEET

CORNBREAD

Bring a touch of the South to your table. This is a sweet cornbread with a nice touch of honey. It's hearty and robust with plenty of cornmeal, but still moist and tender. Generally cornbread recipes advise to not over mix, but with gluten-free flours, the same does not apply. Mix it well and let it stand a bit so the liquids absorb and the cultured dairy has a chance to start breaking down the grains. This quick bread goes nicely with chili, spicy soup, and ribs. Top it with lots of butter and a little honey, and it's almost like a dessert. Never give honey to children under 1 year of age. —Tana

INGREDIENTS

⅓ cup almond flour

¼ cup brown rice flour

¼ cup sorghum flour

2 Tbsp. teff flour

⅓ cup tapioca starch

¼ cup potato starch

1 cup cornmeal

½ tsp. xanthan gum

½ tsp. gelatin

1 tsp. baking soda

2 tsp. baking powder

½ tsp. Real Salt

1¼ cups honey

2 eggs

¼ cup coconut oil

½ cup heavy cream

½ cup buttermilk

 INSTRUCTIONS

Preheat oven to 400 degrees. Stir together all dry ingredients. Combine all wet ingredient together, mix well. Combine wet and dry ingredients and mix well. Let stand for 5–10 minutes.

Scrape batter into a greased 9-inch square baking pan. Bake for 18–20 minutes or until a toothpick in center comes out clean. Don't check until after 16–17 minutes or center may fall.

TANA'S TIPS TAKE IT UP A NOTCH

Honey is a superfood and has many health-promoting properties, plus it is delicious! Buy a raw local honey, as many of the important properties are removed when the honey is heated.

PÃO DE

QUEIJO

Brazilian cheese bread—what can be said but YUM! Early on after starting my gluten-free life, I was intro-duced to these yummy little nuggets at a Brazilian restaurant at a resort in Scottsdale, Arizona. My daughter was working at the resort and said, "Mom, you have to go to this restaurant with me; they have this gluten-free bread that is to die for." That was good enough for me; it had been a while since I'd had anything that even resembled bread. We ate them until our tummies were about to burst and to the dismay of our server, who returned over and over with one roll at a time. Well, I'm a long way from Scottsdale so making Pão de Queijo at home was my only option. These are best right from the oven slathered in butter. —Tana

INGREDIENTS

2 cups tapioca starch

1 Tbsp. sugar

1 tsp. Real Salt

2 tsp. baking powder

2 eggs, beaten

5½ Tbsp. butter, melted

¾ cup whole milk

12 oz. Queso fresco cheese, shredded or crumbled

½ cup Parmesan cheese

 INSTRUCTIONS

Mix all dry ingredients together. Using a stand mixer combine eggs, butter, and milk. On a low speed, blend in the dry ingre-dients. Add both types of cheese and mix for an additional 2 minutes or so. Let the dough rest for 20 minutes.

Heat oven to 400 degrees. With greased hands, roll dough into balls and place them 2 inches apart on a baking pad or a parchment lined cookie sheet. Bake for 20 minutes or until golden brown. Makes 24 rolls.

☞ *delectable desserts*

GRANNY SMITH APPLE CRISP

PISTACHIO CREAM DELIGHT

BLUEBERRY TURNOVERS

BROWN BUTTER SNICKERDOODLES

CHERRY CHIP COOKIES

CHOCOLATE CARAMEL TOFFEE CAKE

ICE CREAM SANDWICHES

LUSCIOUS LEMON CHEESECAKE

BANANA BLACK-BOTTOM PIE

MINT BROWNIES

PEANUT BUTTER BARS

MRS. B'S OATMEAL CHOCOLATE CHIP COOKIES

OLD-FASHIONED STRAWBERRY BARS

POUND CAKE

PUMPKIN SPICE MINI BUNDTS

RHUBARB CRUMBLE

TANGY SWEET LEMON BARS

TRES LECHES

WHATEVER CAKE

SWEET PRETZEL SALAD

PEANUT BUTTER DELIGHTS

POPPY SEED CAKE

APPLE CRISP

Apple crisp is a quick and easy dessert that will impress. We all have a few apples in the fridge at any given time, and you can mix a double or triple batch of the topping up in advance and keep it frozen for a real time saver. Apple crisp can be made at the spur of the moment and everyone will think you've slaved over it for hours. It's also a great way to use up apples that no one will eat because they have softened a bit. —Tana

INGREDIENTS

TOPPING

⅓ cup almond flour

⅓ cup brown rice flour

⅓ cup sorghum flour

1 Tbsp. tapioca starch

½ tsp. baking powder

1 cup certified gluten-free rolled oats

1 cup sugar

¾ cup butter

FILLING

6–7 large Granny Smith apples (any type of apple will work)

1 Tbsp. lemon juice

¾ cup sugar

3 Tbsp. cornstarch

1 tsp. cinnamon

½ tsp. nutmeg

 INSTRUCTIONS

Preheat oven to 350 degrees. Using a stand mixer, cream together butter and sugar. Combine dry ingredients together and add to butter and sugar mixture. Mix until crumbly; do not over mix or topping will become dough-like.

Peel, core, slice, and quarter apples (an apple peeler works great and will save time). Toss in lemon juice to keep them from browning. Pat apples dry with a paper towel and then toss them with sugar, cornstarch, cinnamon, and nutmeg. Place in a 9 × 13 pan or in individual baking dishes. Using your hands, crumble the topping mixture over the apples. Add an additional dash of cinnamon on top.

Bake uncovered for 45–50 minutes. Serve warm with homemade whipped cream or vanilla ice cream.

TANA'S
TIPS
TAKE IT UP A NOTCH

Apples are a high priority fruit to go organic. It's nice that the cost difference between conventional and organic for apples is generally very small.

INSTRUCTIONS

It saves a little time to make the pudding layer first, even though it goes on top of the others, so it has time to cool while making the other layers. The crust layer does not need to be completely cold for the cream cheese layer to be spread on top of it, just cool enough so it doesn't melt it. Also the pudding doesn't have to be completely cold either, again just enough not to melt the cream cheese layer beneath it.

In a medium saucepan, combine 2 cups cream, 1 cup milk, ¾ cup sugar, butter and ground pistachios. Heat until butter is melted and milk is slightly scalded. As the pistachios are cooked they will release their green color. Whisk together egg yolks and ⅓ cups sugar. Slowly add this mixture to the hot mixture, whisking lightly. Continue cooking for 10–15 minutes on a low heat until mixture starts to thicken a bit. Mix reserved milk and cornstarch together. Add to the hot milk mixture, whisking constantly. Intermittently whisk as mixture continues to cook for the next 5–10 minutes. When pudding has thickened, remove from heat and blend in almond extract. Cover with plastic wrap (to avoid skimming) and place in refrigerator to cool while you are making the other layers. When cooled, pour over the cream cheese layer.

Preheat oven to 350 degrees. Combine all dry crust ingredients including almonds and powdered sugar; mix well. Cut butter into small pieces or grate into the dry ingredient. Mix to coat. Add the beaten egg and vanilla and blend until everything is well combined. Press mixture into a greased 9 × 13 baking pan. Bake for 20 minutes. Remove from oven and let cool.

Whip 1 pint of heavy whipping cream with ½ cup powdered sugar until stiff peaks form. Remove 1 cup to use in the cream cheese layer. Reserve the remainder to top the dessert. Cut the cream cheese into small pieces. Add powdered sugar a little at a time into the cream cheese, while you are mixing. When powdered sugar and cream cheese are blended smooth, fold in 1 cup of whipped cream. Spread this layer on top of the cool crust.

Spread the cooled pistachio pudding over the cream cheese layer and refrigerate for a minimum of 2–3 hours. When you are ready to serve, top with the reserved whipped cream.

DELIGHT

Pistachio Cream Delight has always been one of Chandice's favorite desserts and she requested that I come up with a gluten-free version. I wanted to make it, not only gluten-free but with a completely homemade pistachio pudding. There is no comparison in how much better homemade pudding tastes compared to boxed pudding. —Tana

INGREDIENTS

CRUST
¼ cup almond flour

¼ cup brown rice flour

¼ cup sorghum flour

¼ cup white rice flour

½ cup tapioca starch

½ cup potato starch

1 tsp. xanthan gum

1 tsp. baking powder

⅓ cup powdered sugar

¼ cup finely chopped almonds

½ cup butter

1 egg, beaten

1 tsp. gluten-free vanilla

CREAM CHEESE LAYER
2 (8-oz.) pkgs. cream cheese, softened

1 pint heavy whipping cream

½ cup powdered sugar

PISTACHIO PUDDING
2 cups heavy cream

2 cups whole milk, divided

¾ cup sugar

2 Tbsp. butter

¾ cup finely ground pistachios

½ cup sugar

4 egg yolks

6 Tbsp. cornstarch

1 tsp. gluten-free almond extract

TANA'S
TIPS
TAKE IT UP A NOTCH

This recipe requires a large amount of powdered sugar. Try an organic powdered sugar instead.

BLUEBERRY

TURNOVERS

Blueberries aren't my favorite berry, but blueberry is my very favorite fruit filling. It cooks down so nicely, all gooey and sweet, literally bursting with flavor. Paired with a delicious flaky crust, blueberries make these turnovers something to talk about. —Tana

INGREDIENTS

pastry crust recipe (page 224)

BLUEBERRY FILLING
1 (10-oz.) pkg. blueberries
⅓ cup sugar
3 Tbsp. cornstarch
powdered sugar for dusting

INSTRUCTIONS

In a saucepan combine all ingredients except powdered sugar and mix well. Stirring constantly, heat berry mixture on a medium heat until it has thickened. Preheat oven to 400 degrees.

Prepare pie crust. Place plastic wrap on surface and over edge. Shape dough into a rectangular disc. Sprinkle a small amount of white rice flour on top of dough. Roll dough into rectangles. Cut into smaller triangles using a pizza cutter. Move pastry to a non-stick baking sheet or parchment-lined baking pan.

Spoon 2–3 tablespoons of blueberry mixture on bottom half of triangle staying at least ½ inch from the edge. Wet fingers with a small amount of water and run along the edge of the pastry. Fold top half over the bottom and lightly press pastry together along edges. Using the tines of a fork seal the edges on cut sides.

Bake for 19–21 minutes. Let pastries cool slightly and dust with powdered sugar.

BROWN BUTTER

TANA'S
TIPS
TAKE IT UP A NOTCH

Buy an organic butter or at least one without annatto, which is an unnecessary coloring.

⟨ ···SNICKERDOODLES··· ⟩

Snickerdoodles were the first homemade cookie I learned to make. Simple ingredients make them easy and foolproof to prepare. During the summer my sister and I would make them at least twice a week. Using brown butter adds a deep, almost nutty flavor to this classic favorite. —Tana

INGREDIENTS

⅓ cup + 2 Tbsp. almond flour	½ tsp. Real Salt
⅓ cup + 1 Tbsp. brown rice flour	½ tsp. cinnamon
½ cup sorghum flour	1 cup brown sugar
½ cup white rice flour	½ cup sugar
½ cup tapioca starch	1 egg
¼ cup potato starch	2 Tbsp. sour cream
1 Tbsp. arrowroot starch	1 tsp. gluten-free vanilla extract
½ tsp. xanthan gum	1½ cubes butter
2 tsp. baking powder	

FOR ROLLING

⅓ cup sugar

1 tsp. cinnamon

INSTRUCTIONS

In a saucepan over medium heat, melt butter. Continue heating as butter begins to foam, whisking continuously until butter starts to brown and give off a nutty aroma (do not burn). Remove from heat and transfer to another bowl to stop the heating process. Let cool.

In a stand mixer, combine all dry ingredients down to the sugars. Mix together well. Combine cooled butter and both sugars. Add egg, sour cream, and vanilla. Add dry mixture a little at a time while mixing until all ingredients are well incorporated.

Chill dough in refrigerator for 2–3 hours or in freezer for 30 minutes. Preheat oven to 350 degrees. Mix remaining sugar and cinnamon together. Roll dough into balls and then into cinnamon sugar mixture to coat. Place dough balls on cookie sheet a couple inches apart. Bake for 8–10 minutes for a softer cookie, 11–13 minutes for a crispier cookie.

CHERRY CHIP

COOKIES

There used to be a bakery in the town neighboring ours that my mother worked at. They made the best cherry chip cookie ever. Once in a while my mom would take us with her to pick up something and let us choose one treat. I always chose a cherry chip cookie. Eventually the bakery closed and it had been years since I'd had the delight of this cookie. I always checked in any new bakery I found to see if they carried them, with no success. I came across a recipe several years ago that used cranberries, but tasted very much like the cherry chip cookies I remembered. I converted it into a gluten-free version and now my life is complete (just kidding, but these cookies really do help). —Tana

INGREDIENTS

1 cup butter, softened

1½ cups powdered sugar

1 tsp. gluten-free vanilla

1 egg

1½ cups coconut flakes

⅔ cups almond flour

⅓ cup brown rice flour

⅔ cups sorghum flour

⅔ cups white rice flour

⅔ cups tapioca starch

⅓ cup potato starch

1 tsp. baking powder

1½ tsp. xanthan gum

½ tsp. Real Salt

1½ cups cherry chips, cranberries, or mini chocolate chips

 INSTRUCTIONS

Preheat oven to 350 degrees. Using a stand mixture, cream together butter, sugar, vanilla, and egg. Combine all remaining ingredients together except coconut flakes and cherry chips and mix well.

Blend dry ingredients into wet ingredients until well mixed. Add coconut and mix well. Fold in cherry chips. Using a cookie scoop, place dough on a baking sheet and flatten slightly with the back of a spoon. Bake for 12 minutes until edges a lightly browned.

TANA'S TIPS · TAKE IT UP A NOTCH

Try using natural unsweetened coconut in this recipe. These cookies are already very sweet; unsweetened coconut takes it down a bit. You may find that you like these cookies better when they are not quite as sweet.

CHOCOLATE CARAMEL

TANA'S TIPS · TAKE IT UP A NOTCH

All cacao and cocoa powder are not created equal. Use a high quality cacao powder or cocoa powder that is finely milled and processed without alkali. Chocolate is high in antioxidants so eat up and enjoy your chocolate cake!

TOFFEE CAKE

I am not a chocolate lover; in fact, before making this cake I don't ever remember making a chocolate cake. I've made many other cakes, just not chocolate. I quickly realized that I shouldn't be the one to judge this cake, so I called upon my crazy, chocolate-loving sister and sister-in-law to help me decide if this cake was cookbook worthy. After trying it, they informed me that it wasn't just good, it was amazing. My sister told me she had actually dreamed about this cake, it was so good. In addition, I had about 15 other non–gluten-free people try it, and everyone gave it a big thumbs up. With that kind of endorsement, I'll take it that this recipe is a hit with most anyone. Surprisingly, I really liked this cake too; I guess I'll be making chocolate cake more often now. —Tana

INGREDIENTS

¼ cup brown rice flour

¼ cup white rice flour

¼ cup sorghum flour

¼ cup teff flour

½ cup tapioca starch

¼ cup potato starch

¾ tsp. xanthan gum

½ tsp. gelatin

¼ tsp. salt

1½ tsp. baking powder

1 tsp. baking soda

1½ cups sugar

4 eggs

2 tsp. gluten-free vanilla

1 cup sour cream

½ cup butter

⅓ cup coconut oil

¾ cup or 6 oz. semi-sweet chocolate chips

½ cup unsweetened cacao powder

 INSTRUCTIONS

For cake, preheat oven to 350°. Combine all the dry ingredients together and mix well. Using a stand mixer, cream together sugar, eggs and vanilla. After it is well combined, add the sour cream. Add the dry ingredients to the wet creamy mixture a little bit at a time until it is all combined.

Meanwhile, in a small sauce pan, melt butter, coconut oil & chocolate chips. Whisk in cocoa powder after the mixture is melted. Add the chocolate mixture to the other until all the chocolate is incorporated in. Pour cake batter into two 9" greased cake pans.

Bake for 25-27 minutes until a toothpick in center comes out clean (don't open oven door to check until at least 23-24 minutes or your cake may fall). Let cakes cool slightly, then run a knife around the edge and invert into a cooling rack.

CARAMEL SAUCE

& FROSTING

INGREDIENTS

CARAMEL SAUCE
1 cup sugar

¼ cup water

1 stick butter, cut into pieces

½ cup heavy whipping cream

2 tsp. vanilla

FROSTING
1 (8-oz.) pkg. cream cheese, softened

½ cup powdered sugar

1 tsp. vanilla

16 oz. heavy whipping cream

½ cup powdered sugar

 INSTRUCTIONS

For caramel sauce, combine sugar and water in a sauce pan. Turn stove top to a medium-high heat. Stir constantly until sugar is completely dissolved. Cover and boil for 2 minutes. Remove lid and continue boiling until the it starts to turn brown around the edges. Continue stirring and it starts to turn a deep amber color. Remove from heat and whisk in butter until melted. Stir in cream and add vanilla. Cool until slightly warm.

For frosting, combine cream cheese, ½ cup powdered sugar and vanilla together until smooth. In another bowl, whip cream and ½ cup powdered sugar until stiff peaks can form. Fold the two mixtures together.

Place bottom cake on a cake plate, poke 2-3 dozen holes in it with a skewer being careful to not break up the cake. Pour caramel sauce over the holes. Using the back of a spoon, work the caramel into the cake. Pour on more as needed. Frost the top of this cake with about ½"-1" of frosting. Place the second cake on top of it and pokes holes and drench with caramel the same as the first cake, being careful to not poke holes through the frosting and into the bottom layer. After adding caramel to both layers there will be ½ cup or so leftover. Save this for use later as a topping for ice cream or apples. Frost both layers of the cake and top with toffee bits.

INSTRUCTIONS

Preheat oven to 375 degrees. Using a stand mixer, cream together butter, sugar, eggs and vanilla. Mix all dry ingredients except the cacao powder together and blend into the cream mixture. Add cacao powder and mix well. Working in small batches, roll out dough on plastic wrap; use only enough rice flour so rolling pin does not stick. Using a cookie cutter, cut out circles. Remove edges and lift the edge of the plastic and tip the cookies one by one onto your hand, then lay onto a bake sheet or parchment lined cookie sheet. Repeat with remaining dough. Put a decorative top into the cookies with the tines of a fork or with a toothpick. Bake for 9–10 minutes. Let cookies cool completely. Buy a vanilla ice cream that is in a paper container. Cut and peel away paper in strips as you cut off slices of ice cream about 1–1½ inches thick. Place on a cookie sheet and freeze for 30 minutes or so to firm up ice cream. Lay out half of the cookies on a cookie sheet. Using a cookie cutter the same size as the chocolate cookies, cut out circles in the ice cream. Place the ice cream on half the cookies and top with the other half of the cookies. Put sandwiches in the freezer until completely frozen. Wrap any ice cream sandwiches you don't eat immediately to avoid freezer burn.

If you are using this recipe for chocolate cookie crumbs, spread dough out on a lined cookie sheet and bake for 14–15 minutes. Let cool. Make cookie crumbs by adding pieces into a food processor until they are ground into fine crumbs. This recipe will make enough to yield 6–8 ice cream sandwiches and 3 cups of cookie crumbs. Cookie crumbs can also be frozen for later use.

Find a vanilla ice cream with 5 ingredients or less—that is all that are necessary. Avoid any containing high fructose corn syrup.

SANDWICHES

Ice cream sandwiches are a favorite of mine, but I can't see paying two dollars or more for one little sand-wich! Making your own is always the least-expensive option, and you control all the ingredients. They will keep for up to a month in the freezer when well wrapped. So make a big batch and enjoy them as you please, but you might find they disappear quickly because they are so irresistible. —Tana

INGREDIENTS

¼ cup almond flour

¼ cup brown rice flour

¼ cup sorghum flour

¼ cup teff flour

⅓ cup tapioca starch

⅓ cup + 1 Tbsp. potato starch

¾ tsp. xanthan gum

1 tsp. baking powder

¼ tsp. Real Salt

¾ cup cacao powder

¾ cup sugar

8 Tbsp. butter

2 eggs

1½ tsp. gluten-free vanilla

LUSCIOUS LEMON

 INSTRUCTIONS

Store-bought gingersnaps work fine or you can make your own; see the recipe below.

Preheat oven to 350 degrees. Combine cookie crumbs and sugar. Pour melted butter over crumbs and mix together. Press into bottom and up sides of a spring form pan.

Using a stand mixer with the whisk, whip cream cheese, adding in sugar a little at a time. Continue mixing on a low speed while you add eggs, one at a time. Mix until smooth. Stir in lemon juice. Pour filling into crust. Bake for approximately 45 minutes.

Whip sour cream, powdered sugar and vanilla together. Spread on the top of the cheesecake and return to the oven. Bake for an additional 10 minutes. Cool before removing side from spring form pan. Refrigerate until ready to serve. Garnish with whipped cream and lemon slices.

For cookies, preheat oven to 375 degrees. Using a stand mixer, cream together butter, sugar, eggs, and vanilla. Mix all dry ingredients together and blend into the cream mixture. Spread dough out on a lined cookie sheet and bake for 14–15 minutes. Let cool. Make cookie crumbs by adding pieces into a food processor until they are ground into fine crumbs. Cookie crumbs can also be frozen for later use.

TANA'S
TIPS
TAKE IT UP A NOTCH

Bottled lemon and lime juices usually contain preservatives as well as additional ingredients like oil to prolong shelf life. Opt for a fresh-pressed, not-from-concentrate juice. The fresh lemon taste is amazing!

CHEESECAKE

Lemon, lemon, lemon … I love lemon anything! Cheesecake is usually a rich, heavy dessert (which I do love at times) suited more for winter time, but adding the luscious lemon and putting it on a gingersnap crust makes it a great dessert for summer time too. This lemon cheesecake is smooth and creamy with just the right zest. It's a great way to switch up your regular cheesecake routine. —Tana

INGREDIENTS

GINGERSNAP CRUST

3 cups gluten-free gingersnap cookie crumbs

¾ cup butter, melted

3 Tbsp. sugar

LEMON CREAM FILLING

4 (8-oz.) pkgs. cream cheese

4 eggs

2 cups sugar

½ cup lemon juice

16 oz. sour cream

3 Tbsp. powdered sugar

½ tsp. gluten-free vanilla

GINGERSNAP COOKIES OR COOKIE CRUMBS

¼ cup almond flour

¼ cup brown rice flour

¼ cup sorghum flour

¼ cup teff flour

⅓ cup tapioca starch

½ cup potato starch

¾ tsp. xanthan gum

1 tsp. baking powder

¼ tsp. Real Salt

¾ cup sugar

¼ cup molasses

4 Tbsp. butter

1 egg

2 tsp. cinnamon

2 tsp. ground ginger

INSTRUCTIONS

Preheat oven to 375 degrees. Combine cookie crumbs and sugar. Pour melted butter over crumbs and mix together. Press into bottom and up sides of a spring form pan. Bake for 8–10 minutes.

In a saucepan heat chocolate chips and cream until melted, stirring constantly. Pour into cookie crumb crust. Let cool. If you would like a thicker ganache add more in 2 to 1 ratios.

In a saucepan on low heat, heat milk (remember to reserve 1 cup), cream, sugar (¾ cup), and butter. Cream together egg yolks and remaining sugar (½ cup). Whisk into hot cream mixture. Allow mixture to cook, stirring frequently, until it starts to thicken. Make sure heat is very low. Mix reserved milk and cornstarch together. Slowly whisk into the hot mixture. Whisking constantly, making sure to blend bottom and sides, and continue cooking until mixture is a thick pudding. Remove from heat. As the pudding starts to cool, place plastic wrap on top to avoid filming. Continue cooling in fridge.

Slice bananas and toss with lemon juice. Pat dry with a paper towel. Line bananas on top of cooled ganache. Pour cooled pudding over bananas and place in fridge to continue cooling. When ready to serve, prepare whipped cream by adding all ingredients together and whipping until soft firm. Spread whipped cream over pudding, garnish with grated chocolate and strawberries or other fruit if desired. Remove sides of spring form pan and slide pie from bottom onto a serving plate.

If a spring form pan is not available this dessert can be made in two 9-inch pie pans by dividing all ingredients equally between the two.

TANA'S TIPS — TAKE IT UP A NOTCH

Use an organic, grass-fed whole milk and heavy whipping cream. It is a fantastic way to turn less desirable fat into good fat in this amazing pie. See more info in the "The Greatest Wealth is Health" section.

PIE

Years ago, before my gluten-free life, I used to enjoy the most luscious banana black-bottom pie for dessert at my favorite restaurant, Snake Creek Grill. Instead of resigning myself to never enjoying it again, I decided to create my own gluten-free rendition. It works out to be a lot cheaper than the $7 a slice restaurant version and tastes just as amazing. This dessert is one of three or four treats my family, extended family, and friends (the majority of whom are not gluten-free) ask for repeatedly. My gluten-free version makes it a dessert the whole family can enjoy! —Tana

INGREDIENTS

COOKIE CRUST

3 cups gluten-free crushed chocolate wafer cookies (page 167)

4 Tbsp. sugar

¾ cup butter, melted

GANACHE

8 oz. chocolate chips

4 oz. heavy whipping cream

BANANA PUDDING

2 cups milk, divided

2 cups heavy whipping cream

¾ cup sugar

2 Tbsp. butter

4 egg yolks

½ cup sugar

6 Tbsp. cornstarch

1 tsp. gluten-free banana extract

2–3 bananas

1 Tbsp. lemon juice

WHIPPED CREAM

16 oz. heavy whipping cream

½ cup powdered sugar

1 tsp. gluten-free vanilla

small chocolate bar and fruit to garnish

MINT

BROWNIES

I think brownies should be very dense and moist, perfectly balanced between fudge and cake. That's why it's called something different—a brownie. These brownies are just the right balance, chewy and gooey. I love the added flavor of cool mint in the filling and frosting—so it's not just a plain brownie. —Tana

INGREDIENTS

BROWNIE
¼ cup almond flour
¼ cup sorghum flour
¼ cup teff flour
¼ cup tapioca starch
¼ cup potato starch
½ cup cacao powder
½ tsp. xanthan gum
½ tsp. gelatin
⅛ tsp. Real Salt
2 cups sugar
½ cup coconut oil
5 eggs

MINT FILLING
2 cups powdered sugar
½ cup butter, softened
1 Tbsp. milk
½ tsp. gluten-free mint extract

CHOCOLATE TOPPING
2 cups chocolate chips
8 Tbsp. butter
1 tsp. mint extract

INSTRUCTIONS

Preheat oven to 350 degrees. Using a stand mixer, cream together sugar and coconut oil. Mix in eggs one at a time. Combine all the remaining dry ingredients together except the cacao powder. Add to the cream mixture and mix well. Add the cacao powder and blend in well. Let sit for 5–10 minutes.

Pour batter into a greased a 9 × 13 baking pan. Bake for 30 minutes. Cool completely on a wire rack. Combine all filling ingredients and mix together until smooth and creamy. Spread over the top of the cooled brownies. Refrigerate for a few minutes to set while making chocolate topping.

In a small saucepan, melt chocolate chips and butter. When completely melted add mint extract and blend in well. Let cool for 30 minutes or more, until barely warm. Spread chocolate topping over the filling. Chill thoroughly before cutting into squares. Store in the refrigerator.

TANA'S TIPS — TAKE IT UP A NOTCH

Coconut oil gives baked goods an amazing flavor and texture. It is also very nutritious; try replacing oils in other recipes with coconut oil.

Many peanut butters contain hydrogenated oil. Find a natural peanut butter, one in which the oil separates to the top. You will love the fresh roasted peanut butter taste.

BARS

These bars take me back to my days in elementary school. Our lunch ladies made the most wonderful peanut butter bars ever. It always made math a little easier when I could smell the aroma of peanut butter drifting through the hallways and I knew I would be getting my favorite peanut butter bar very shortly. My gluten-free version is just as memorable. —Tana

INGREDIENTS

⅓ cup almond flour

⅓ cup brown rice flour

⅓ cup sorghum flour

¼ cup teff flour

⅓ cup tapioca starch

¼ cup potato starch

1 tsp. baking soda

½ tsp. Real Salt

¾ cup butter

¾ cup sugar

¾ cup brown sugar

2 eggs

1 tsp. gluten-free vanilla

¾ cup peanut butter, creamy or crunchy

1 ½ cups certified gluten-free oats

PEANUT BUTTER FROSTING

½ cup powdered sugar

¼ cup creamy peanut butter

2–4 Tbsp. milk

CHOCOLATE FROSTING

1 cup chocolate chips

¼ cup butter

INSTRUCTIONS

Preheat oven to 350 degrees. Using a stand mixer, cream together butter and sugar. Add eggs and vanilla and mix well. Blend in peanut butter. Combine remaining dry ingredients except oats and mix them into the cream mixture a little at a time. Add the oats and blend well. Spread into a large, greased 10 × 14 baking pan. Bake for 20 minutes. Let cool for 20 minutes or so.

Prepare peanut butter frosting by whisking together peanut butter and milk. Add in powdered sugar and mix until smooth and creamy. Spread on top of peanut butter bars.

Prepare chocolate frosting by melting butter and chocolate chips together in a small saucepan. Drizzle chocolate frosting on top of the peanut butter frosting. Using a butter knife cut the peanut butter and chocolate frosting together to make a decorative pattern. Let bars cool completely before cutting.

MRS. B'S OATMEAL

CHOCOLATE CHIP COOKIES

Everyone loves a great chocolate chip cookie. Mrs. Somebody Else has even made a successful business of it. This is my gluten-free version of the cookie that made her famous. This recipe makes a big batch, so hopefully you will get to enjoy a few baked cookies,.I usually only end up with about half because I love eating the dough so much. Sometimes I don't bake any; I just freeze what is left in ready-to-go balls, thinking I might bake them another day. It never happens, but we do get a nice cold little treat every day for a week. —Tana

INGREDIENTS

- ½ lb. butter
- ½ cup sugar
- 1 cup brown sugar
- 1 Tbsp. gluten-free vanilla
- 2 eggs
- ¾ cup almond flour
- ½ cup brown rice flour
- ¼ cup sorghum flour
- ½ cup teff flour
- ½ cup tapioca starch
- ½ tsp. xanthan gum
- ½ tsp. gelatin
- 1 tsp. baking powder
- 1 tsp. baking soda
- 2½ cups certified gluten-free oats
- ½–1 cup chocolate chips
- ½–1 cup chopped nuts

 INSTRUCTIONS

Preheat oven to 350 degrees. Using a stand mixer, cream together butter and sugar. Add eggs one at a time and mix well. Add vanilla. Combine all remaining dry ingredients except oats, chocolate chips, and nuts. Mix into the creamed ingredients a little at a time.

Add the oats and blend in completely. Fold in chocolate chips and nuts. Scoop dough onto a baking pad or greased cookie sheet. Bake for 11–13 minutes, or longer if you like your cookie crispier.

TANA'S
TIPS
TAKE IT UP A NOTCH

If you plan to eat dough, make sure your eggs are organic pastured farm-fresh or leave the eggs out and just eat all the dough, to avoid any chance of pathogens.

STRAWBERRY BARS

These old-time bars really need to make a comeback in today's world. They are moist and chewy, filled with flavorful strawberry preserves. My very picky nephew gobbled these up in no time. —Tana

INGREDIENTS

½ cup brown rice flour

½ cup white rice flour

⅓ cup sorghum flour

¼ cup teff flour

½ cup tapioca starch

½ cup potato starch

1 tsp. xanthan gum

½ tsp. baking powder

½ cup sugar

½ cup brown sugar

1 cup butter

1 egg

1 cup chopped nuts

1 (10-oz.) jar strawberry jam

¼ cup certified gluten-free oats

 INSTRUCTIONS

Preheat oven to 350 degrees. Using a stand mixer, cream together sugar, butter, and eggs. Combine the top 8 dry ingredient together. Add to the cream mixture. Add the nuts and mix in well. Remove 1½ cup of the mixture and save for topping. Press remaining mixture into a 8-inch square baking pan. Spread jam to within ½ inch from edge.

Add oats to the reserved mixture and crumble over the preserves. Bake for 40 minutes or until lightly browned. Cool completely before cutting into bars. You can substitute your favorite flavor of jam for the strawberry jam.

TANA'S
TIPS
TAKE IT UP A NOTCH

Use a jam or preserve that has no added sugar. The fruit on its own is plenty sweet.

POUND

CAKE

Pound cake is supposed to be heavy, but many gluten-free pound cakes are as dense as a brick and dry. This pound cake has just the right amount of moisture and crumb, heavy but not dense. Pound cake has always been my favorite type of cake (though my chocolate cake recipe in this book might be challenging that spot). I love the buttery flavor with just a hint of lemon, topped with whipped cream and berries, it makes a delightful summer dessert. —Tana

INGREDIENTS

¼ cup almond flour

⅓ cup brown rice flour

¼ cup sorghum flour

2 Tbsp. coconut flour

½ cup tapioca starch

½ cup potato starch

½ tsp. xanthan gum

2 tsp. baking powder

1 cup sugar

½ cup butter, softened

4 eggs

1 Tbsp. lemon juice

2 tsp. gluten-free vanilla extract

GLAZE

2 Tbsp. butter, melted

1 Tbsp. lemon juice

1 Tbsp. milk

1 cup powdered sugar

INSTRUCTIONS

Preheat oven to 350 degrees. Grease a loaf pan with coconut oil or butter. Using a stand mixer, cream together butter and sugar until very light and fluffy. Mix in eggs one at a time, then add vanilla and lemon juice. Continue blending until mixture is frothy and light.

Combine all other dry ingredients and mix well. Add the dry mixture a little at a time until well mixed and light. Pour batter into a greased loaf pan and bake for 45–60 minutes or until a toothpick in the center comes out clean. Do not open oven to test doneness until at least 45 minutes or cake may fall in the center. Let cake cool slightly.

Prepare glaze by adding all ingredients together and whisking until smooth. Drizzle over the top and sides of the pound cake. When cake is completely cooled, slice and top with real whipped cream and fresh strawberries or other fruit of your choice.

PUMPKIN SPICE

MINI BUNDTS

These mini bundts are especially delicious during the fall harvest time. They are soft and tender with a light pumpkin flavor, subtly spiced with cinnamon and ginger. The maple nut frosting adds the finishing touch.
—Tana

INGREDIENTS

⅓ cup almond flour

3 Tbsp. brown rice flour

¼ cup sorghum flour

⅓ cup teff flour

2 Tbsp. coconut flour

½ cup tapioca starch

¼ cup potato starch

½ tsp. xanthan gum

1 cup packed brown sugar

1 tsp. baking powder

1 tsp. baking soda

½ tsp. Real Salt

1 tsp. cinnamon

¼ tsp. ginger

¼ cup nutmeg

½ cup butter, melted

½ cup cooked or canned pumpkin

⅓ cup buttermilk

2 eggs, beaten

MAPLE FROSTING

1 Tbsp. butter, melted

¼ cup maple syrup

1 cup powdered sugar

¼–⅓ cup finely chopped nuts

 INSTRUCTIONS

Preheat oven to 375 degrees. Stir together all dry ingredients, including sugar and spices. Using a stand mixer, combine remaining 4 wet ingredients.

Add dry mixture a little at a time, and stir until moistened. Let batter rest for 5–10 minutes. Spoon batter into greased mini bundt molds or a muffin pan. Bake for 17–18 minutes. Combine all frosting ingredients, except nuts, and mix well. Fold in nuts. Drizzle over cooled bundt cakes.

TANA'S TIPS TAKE IT UP A NOTCH

Fresh nutmeg has an amazing aroma and flavor; switch out fresh grated for powdered.

RHUBARB

CRUMBLE

We always had a big rhubarb plant when I was growing up. I used to love picking a stalk and eating it with a big sprinkle of salt. Many times my mother would make rhubarb crumble from it during the summer. I was so excited when we bought our house and we noticed they had planted rhubarb. It has been growing for more than 20 years in our yard and for 20 summers I have made rhubarb crumble more than any other dessert. As the plant has grown (it's 5–6 feet in diameter now) we can't keep up eating it, so I freeze several quarts every year. This way we can enjoy this family favorite dessert year round. Serve with vanilla ice cream—it's the best! —Tana

INGREDIENTS

6 cups rhubarb

1 cup sugar

2 Tbsp. cornstarch

TOPPING

⅓ cup almond flour

⅓ cup brown rice flour

⅓ cup sorghum flour

1 Tbsp. tapioca starch

½ tsp. baking powder

1 cup certified gluten-free rolled oats

1 cup sugar

¾ cup butter

 INSTRUCTIONS

Preheat oven to 350 degrees. Using a stand mixer, cream together butter and sugar. Combine dry ingredients together and add to butter and sugar mixture. Mix until crumbly. Do not over mix or topping will become dough-like.

If you are using frozen rhubarb, just mix it with the sugar and cornstarch. For fresh rhubarb (have the kids go out and pick it), wash and slice it, add sugar and cornstarch and place in a 9 × 13 pan. Using your hands, crumble the topping mixture over the rhubarb.

Bake uncovered for 45–50 minutes. Serve warm topped with vanilla ice cream (I had to get that in twice because it really is the best way!)

TANA'S TIPS TAKE IT UP A NOTCH

Rhubarb is hearty and super easy to grow. It takes almost no time to care for and the rewards are plenty. So if you have even a small space in your yard (it may even work in a large container), get yourself a rhubarb plant. You can make so many things from it and it's really unlikely you will kill it; we haven't!

TANGY SWEET

LEMON BARS

Who can resist a tangy sweet and gooey lemon bar? Not me! These lemon bars really hit the spot for both sweet and tart. They have crisp flaky shortbread crust and a thick layer of that sweet tang! Dusted with powdered sugar they make the perfect summer treat. —Tana

INGREDIENTS

CRUST
¼ cup almond flour
¼ cup brown rice flour
¼ cup sorghum flour
¼ cup white rice flour
½ cup tapioca starch
½ cup potato starch
1 tsp. xanthan gum
1 tsp. baking powder
½ cup powdered sugar
½ cup butter
1 egg, beaten

FILLING
6 eggs
2 cups sugar
½ cup + 1 Tbsp. lemon juice
6 Tbsp. cornstarch
1 tsp. baking powder

 INSTRUCTIONS

Preheat oven to 350 degrees. Combine all dry crust ingredients including powdered sugar, mix well. Cut butter into small pieces or grate into the dry ingredient. Mix to coat. Add the beaten egg and blend until everything is well combined. Press mixture into a greased 9 × 13 baking pan. Bake for 20 minutes. Remove from oven and let cool slightly.

Lightly whisk eggs, sugar and lemon juice together. Add cornstarch and baking powder. Whisk lightly together; do not mix a lot of air into the filling. Pour on top of crust and bake for 30–35 minutes. Allow bars to cool slightly and dust with powdered sugar. Cut into squares and enjoy!

TRES

TANA'S
TIPS
TAKE IT UP A NOTCH

Make your own evaporated milk. Put 2½ cups milk in a medium saucepan. Bring to a boil, turn down heat and simmer until milk has been reduced to 1 cup.

LECHES

Yummy Mexican milk cake. *Tres* is three and *leches* is milk. This cake has three types of milk soaked into the spongy cake. My cake is not like most Americanized tres leches; it is heavier and more spongy. My son, who lived in Guatemala for two years, says this is exactly like authentic Guatemalan tres leches. Make sure to refrigerate this cake for at least 8 hours, because the colder it gets, the better it tastes. —Tana

INGREDIENTS

CAKE

⅓ cup sorghum flour

⅓ cup coconut flour

1 cup white rice flour

½ cup tapioca starch

½ cup potato starch

⅓ cup cornstarch

1 tsp. gelatin

1 Tbsp. baking powder

1 tsp. Real Salt

2 cups sugar

½ cup butter, softened

½ cup coconut oil, softened

1 tsp. gluten-free vanilla

1½ cups milk

6 eggs

TRES LECHES SYRUP

2 (14-oz.) cans sweetened condensed milk

1 cup evaporated milk

1 cup heavy whipping cream

TOPPING

1 cup heavy whipping cream

⅓ cup powdered sugar

dash of cinnamon

dash of nutmeg

INSTRUCTIONS

Preheat oven to 350 degrees. Using a stand mixer, cream together sugar, butter, coconut oil, and vanilla. Continue mixing and add one egg at a time until well mixed. Add milk and mix well. In another bowl, combine the remaining dry ingredients. Add a cup at a time to the creamy mixture until well blended. Grease a 9 × 13 baking pan, pour batter into pan and bake for approximately 45 minutes. Cool partially.

Combine the ingredients for the tres leche syrup. Blend together until smooth. Use a wooden skewer to poke 2–3 dozen holes throughout the cake. Make sure to poke holes along the edges. Pour the syrup over the cake, wait to let the syrup soak in, and then pour on more until all the syrup is on the cake. Cover and refrigerate for 8 hours or overnight.

Add the powdered sugar to the remaining cup of cream and whip lightly. Spread the whipping cream over the top and sprinkle with a little nutmeg and cinnamon. Cut cake into squares and serve with a large spoon to gather the syrup at the bottom of the pan. Store in the refrigerator.

WHATEVER

CAKE

You might ask where is cake got its unusual name. As I was explaining to people what was in this cake I kept saying the phrase, "or whatever you want." We have many ideas and uses for leftovers in this book, but mainly they are for using meat, potatoes, and vegetables. This cake is your answer for leftover fruit and certain veggies. Use the cake as a base and add 2 cups of whatever else you have. For instance, in this particular cake I used crushed pineapple and pumpkin. Sounds like an odd combination, but it was very good. Try a few different combinations to use up your leftovers. How about peaches and carrots, or applesauce and zucchini, or fruit cocktail and bananas? You get the idea. So now you see, it really is a whatever cake. —Tana

INGREDIENTS

⅓ cup almond flour

½ cup brown rice flour

½ cup sorghum flour

1 Tbsp. coconut flour

½ cup tapioca starch

½ cup potato starch

¼ tsp. xanthan gum

2 tsp. baking powder

1 tsp. baking soda

1 cup sugar

1 cup brown sugar

¼ cup coconut oil or butter

2 eggs

1 tsp. gluten-free vanilla

2 cups whatever you want!

 INSTRUCTIONS

Preheat oven to 350 degrees. Make sure the "whatever" has been blended or puréed (adding a little water if it's a drier item), unless is it already pretty smooth, like applesauce or crushed pineapple.

Using a stand mixer, cream together sugar, coconut oil, and eggs. Add vanilla and the "whatever." Combine all dry ingredients together. Add a little at a time into the wet ingredients. Mix until well blended. Pour into a greased 9 × 13 baking pan or two 9-inch cake pans.

Bake for 28–35 minutes until a toothpick in center comes out clean. Serve with frosting of your choice. Frosting pictured is on page 162 (Chocolate Caramel Toffee Cake).

SWEET PRETZEL

SALAD

My step-mom always made this delicious dessert for me growing up. After I was diagnosed with celiac disease, she was sweet enough to help me make it gluten-free. Thanks, Mama Sheila! —Chandice

INGREDIENTS

2 cups gluten-free pretzels

4 Tbsp. sugar

¾ cup melted butter

1 (8-oz.) pkg. cream cheese

1 cup sugar

4 oz. whipping cream

½ cup powdered sugar

1 (6-oz.) pkg. strawberry gelatin

2 cup boiling water

2½ cups sliced fresh or frozen strawberries

 INSTRUCTIONS

Crush pretzels into small pieces. Lay them on a baking sheet and bake at 300 degrees for 5 minutes just to dry them out a little bit. After they are done baking, combine the pretzel crumbs with 4 tablespoons sugar and the melted butter. Press into a 9 × 13 baking pan and bake 15 minutes at 350 degrees.

In a bowl, beat the whipping cream and powdered sugar until stiff peaks form. Meanwhile, mix the cream cheese and remaining sugar. Add that mixture to the whipped cream. Spread on COOLED pretzel crust. In another bowl, combine strawberry gelatin, boiling water, and strawberries.

Let it sit for about 5 minutes or until it begins to look like traditional formed gelatin. This is so that it doesn't just seep down through the cream cheese mixture when poured on, so be sure to wait longer if needed. Pour on top of cream cheese mixture and refrigerate.

TANA'S **TIPS** TAKE IT UP A NOTCH

You could make your own homemade Jello with fruit juice and gelatin

DELIGHTS

These gluten-free peanut butter cookies only have three ingredients. They are so easy to make and taste heavenly! You will love them as much as our family does. We make them every year for our annual Lake Powell trip and they are gobbled down the first day. —Chandice

INGREDIENTS

1 cup peanut butter

½ cup sugar

1 egg

 INSTRUCTIONS

Mix all ingredients with your hands until well combined and roll into balls. Cross press the top of each cookie ball with a fork pushing down into a disc. Bake at 325 degrees for 18–20 minutes.

POPPY SEED

CAKE

This cake was one of the best things I remember eating growing up. When I would visit, my Mama Sheila would let us eat it with milk for breakfast…what a treat! I now do the same for my boys and they get so excited to have cake for breakfast. Thanks to Grammy Sheila for this fun tradition and to Grammy Tana for helping me make it from scratch gluten-free! —Chandice

INGREDIENTS

2½ cups sugar

¼ cup cornstarch

½ tsp. salt

¼ cup sorghum flour

⅔ cup white rice flour

⅔ cup brown rice flour

2 Tbsp. coconut flour

1 Tbsp. baking powder

¼ tsp. baking soda

⅛ tsp. cream of tartar

1½ tsp. xanthan gum

1 tsp. gelatin

1 cup water

½ cup oil

4 eggs

2 Tbsp. gluten-free vanilla extract

2 Tbsp. gluten-free almond extract

2 Tbsp. poppy seeds

INSTRUCTIONS

Preheat oven to 350 degrees. Mix together everything but the poppy seeds, making sure not to over mix. Stir the poppy seeds in at the end gently by hand. Butter and sugar the bottom of a bundt or angel food cake pan.

Pour the cake mix in and bake for 35–45 minutes or until a toothpick entered in the center comes out clean. Let the cake cool then gently remove from the pan and enjoy with a cold glass of milk.

☞ holidays & traditions

Love
ROMANTIC VALENTINE'S DAY DINNER

MEXICAN WEDDING COOKIES

Lucky
SOFT, FLUFFY SUGAR COOKIES WITH CREAM CHEESE FROSTING

Faith
YUMMY POTATOES, HAM, AND PARSLEY CARROTS

Patriotic
SUMMER BBQ RIBS WITH COLE SLAW (TWO WAYS) AND HOMEMADE FRIES & FRY SAUCE

AMERICAN FLAG COOKIE PIZZA

Spooky
SPOOKY SANDWICHES AND CARAMEL CORN

Thankful
GREEN BEAN CASSEROLE WITH HOMEMADE FRIED ONIONS

CANDIED SWEET POTATOES

APPLE PIE

PECAN PIE

CHERRY PIE WITH LATTICE TOP

COCONUT CREAM PIE

Joy
CHRISTMAS EVE TRADITIONS: GINGERBREAD MEN, EGGNOG, AND HOT COCOA

BELGIAN WAFFLES

Celebrate
CELEBRATION CUPCAKES

This gluten-free oatmeal meatloaf is a favorite in our house. It is so easy to make using certified gluten-free oats and just a few other ingredients. I highly recommend using gluten-free Prairie brand oats as they are the best available in my opinion. This meatloaf is a healthier version of a traditional recipe and can easily be shaped into hearts for a delicious, themed meal. We serve it with creamy, cheesy scalloped potatoes and finish it off with romantic chocolate dipped strawberries for a meal that will satisfy but not weigh you down for the rest of the evening. —Chandice

INGREDIENTS

OATMEAL MEATLOAF

1 lb. ground beef

1 egg

¼ cup gluten-free ketchup

1 tsp. gluten-free Worcestershire sauce

2 Tbsp. diced onion

½ cup water

1 cup certified gluten-free oats

1 Tbsp. Italian herbs

1 tsp. Real Salt

½ tsp. black pepper

 INSTRUCTIONS

Mix all ingredients by hand and press down into a loaf pan or shape into hearts and place in a 9 × 13 pan at least 3 inches apart. Bake 1 hour at 350 degrees. Top with more ketchup and broil 3–5 minutes.

DAY DINNER

INGREDIENTS

SCALLOPED POTATOES

2 large russet potatoes, sliced thin

1 Tbsp. butter

1½ cups whole milk

1 cup Parmesan

2 cups shredded cheddar cheese

6 slices Swiss cheese

1 tsp. Real Salt

1 tsp. black pepper

 INSTRUCTIONS

Heat the butter and milk in a saucepan until it begins to boil. Remove from heat and stir in the cheddar and ¾ cup Parmesan. Add the salt and pepper and continue stirring until all the cheese is melted.

Spread ½ cup sauce on the bottom of a 9 × 13 pan, then top with a layer of potatoes. Spread more sauce over the potatoes, making sure to cover them. Continue to layer potatoes and sauce. Between the last two layers of potatoes, layer the slices of Swiss cheese. On the top of the last layer of potatoes and sauce, sprinkle the remaining ¼ cup Parmesan and bake at 325 degrees for 45 minutes.

INGREDIENTS

CHOCOLATE-DIPPED STRAWBERRIES

6 large strawberries

¾ cup milk chocolate chips

¼ cup heavy cream

 INSTRUCTIONS

Wash and thoroughly dry the strawberries. Fill a small saucepan with water to half full. Top with a glass bowl that sits on top without sinking into the water. In that bowl, combine the milk chocolate chips and cream. Heat the pan and stir the chocolate until melted. Remove from heat and dip each strawberry in the chocolate, making sure to cover by twisting.

❬ ··· COOKIES ··· ❭

These wedding cookies are, hands down, one of our favorite cookies of all time. This recipe couldn't be easier and the outcome is just airy, sweet goodness. They make a wonderful addition to any baby or bridal shower with their light texture and appearance. —Chandice

INGREDIENTS

½ cup butter

2 Tbsp. sugar

1 tsp. gluten-free vanilla extract

⅓ cup potato starch

¼ cup tapioca starch

¼ cup almond flour

3 Tbsp. brown rice flour

dash of Real Salt

1 cup finely chopped pecans

powdered sugar for dusting

INSTRUCTIONS

Preheat oven to 300 degrees. Cream the butter, vanilla, and sugar together. In another bowl mix flours and salt, and then add it to the butter mixture. Stir in the pecans.

Roll into 1-inch balls and place on a baking sheet. Bake for 45 minutes. Roll in powdered sugar while warm. Cool, then roll in sugar again.

SOFT, FLUFFY SUGAR COOKIES

Chandice and I have always been friends in food (even during her crazy teenage years); actually, more of accomplices in food. We start making sugar cookies cut into heart shapes on Valentine's, but have to make them again with green frosting on St. Patrick's Day and often again at Easter because the memory of them still lingers. I always make a big batch, because they go fast. We would tell ourselves that we could have one a day until they were gone. However after eating our allotted "one" we would look at each other and one of us would say, "Do you want to split one more?" After that half, we would then say, "Let's split another half." So we would each eat a quarter of a cookie but that left a half of a cookie and why do that, so we would say, "Don't you think we should just split that other half instead of leaving it?" Yes! So in the end we both usually ended up eating 2–3 cookies, just a half and a quarter of a cookie at a time! We still laugh about it and still do the same thing when she and I are together with sugar cookies (for some reason it's just with the sugar cookies). I was determined to create a gluten-free sugar cookie that was exactly the same in flavor and texture. I would not settle in any way on this. They had to be good enough that we would continue to be tempted into eating half and quarter cookies! We couldn't lose the tradition; I think this became more of a tradition than making the cookies for the holiday! Well here it is, they are still thick, fluffy and soft, not too sweet, with lots of cream cheese frosting and yes, they still tempt us! Wanna split a cookie? —Tana

INGREDIENTS

1 cup almond flour

½ cup brown rice flour

½ cup sorghum flour

1 cup white rice flour

1 cup tapioca starch

1 cup potato starch

1 tsp. xanthan gum

2 tsp. baking powder

1 tsp. baking soda

1 cup powdered sugar

1 cup butter, softened

1 cup sour cream

1 egg

2 tsp. gluten-free vanilla

CREAM CHEESE FROSTING

1 (8-oz.) pkg. cream cheese, softened

1 Tbsp. milk

1 Tbsp. gluten-free vanilla

2½ cups powdered sugar

TANA'S TIPS — TAKE IT UP A NOTCH

Use a natural food coloring to tint your frosting.

WITH CREAM CHEESE FROSTING

 INSTRUCTIONS

Preheat oven to 375 degrees. Using a stand mixer, blend together butter and powdered sugar. Add in the sour cream, egg, and vanilla; mix until blended. Combine all remaining dry ingredients together. On the lowest speed (or turn on/off), add the dry mixture one cup at a time. Dough will be thick and barely sticky. Divide dough into quarters. Lay out some plastic wrap and dust lightly with rice flour. Roll out one portion of the dough to ½–⅝ inch thick. You want them thick. Using a cookie cutter, cut into the desired shape, placing the cutter as close as possible so very little dough remains unused. Lift the edge of the plastic wrap and invert cookie onto your hand. Place on a baking pad or parchment-lined cookie sheet. Repeat the process with remaining portions of dough. Bake for 10 minutes. Let cookies cool completely before frosting. To make frosting, whisk together cream cheese, milk, and vanilla. Add in powdered sugar a little at a time and mix until frosting is thick and smooth. Add a drop or two of coloring (optional) and mix well. Frost cooled cookies with a thick layer of frosting. Store in refrigerator and enjoy dipped in a big glass of cold milk.

YUMMY POTATOES, HAM,

We always enjoyed this comforting meal for Easter. The gooey, cheesy potatoes are so delicious that even those who aren't potato fans will find themselves going back for seconds. The carrots complete the meal with "what bunnies like to eat," making it perfect for the holiday. —Chandice

INGREDIENTS

YUMMY POTATOES

1 (32-oz.) bag gluten-free frozen hash browns

1½ cups homemade gluten-free cream of chicken soup (page 80)

2 cups sour cream

1½ cups grated cheddar cheese

⅓ cup melted butter

½ cup chopped onion

1 tsp. Real Salt

1 tsp. black pepper

2 cups crushed gluten-free rice cereal or bread crumbs

2 Tbsp. melted butter

 INSTRUCTIONS

In a large bowl combine hash browns, soup, sour cream, cheese, ⅓ cups butter, salt, pepper, and onion. If it is too dry, add a little extra soup. Place in a 9 × 13 baking dish. In another bowl, combine crushed cereal or bread crumbs and 2 tablespoons melted butter, and then spread over potatoes. Bake at 350 degrees for 40–45 minutes.

AND PARSLEY CARROTS

INGREDIENTS

HAM
1 (10-lb.) gluten-free ham
3 cups water
¾ cup brown sugar
1 tsp. ground cloves

 INSTRUCTIONS

Preheat the oven to 350 degrees. Place ham flat-side down in a roasting pan and pour water around it. In a bowl, combine brown sugar and ground cloves and mix together with your hands. Rub brown sugar mixture into ham, making sure to get it in the sliced creases. Bake for 3½ hours or about 22 minutes per pound. It is done when an internal meat thermometer reads 160 degrees.

INGREDIENTS

PARSLEY CARROTS
2 small bags baby carrots
2 Tbsp. butter
1½ tsp. parsley
Real Salt to taste

 INSTRUCTIONS

Place all ingredients in a saucepan over low to medium heat. Cover and let cook, making sure to stir often, until carrots can be pierced easily with a fork.

SUMMER BBQ RIBS WITH COLESLAW (TWO WAYS)

This combination makes for a great summer meal. Soft tender ribs taste fantastic with this spicy sweet BBQ sauce. Store-bought sauces contain so many undesirable ingredients and they are very expensive. When you make your own homemade sauce you get just the right balance of sweet, spice, and tang because you control the ingredients. Add a little more honey if you want or spice it up with a little more hot sauce. Two types of cole slaw add great variety—they contain the same veggies but they taste nothing alike. Frozen store-bought or drive-through fries are no match for homemade French fries, and no worries—you can make your own sauce for these too. —Tana

INGREDIENTS

2 racks baby back ribs (any type of rib would work)

Real Salt, onion salt, and pepper

BBQ SAUCE

1½ cups gluten-free ketchup

½ cup brown sugar

1 Tbsp. gluten-free Worcestershire sauce

1 tsp. Cholula or other hot sauce

2 Tbsp. apple cider vinegar

¼ cup honey

1 Tbsp. cornstarch

1 Tbsp. dried minced onion

½ tsp. minced garlic

¼ tsp. red pepper flakes

1 tsp. mesquite powder

½ tsp. onion salt

½ tsp. pepper

INSTRUCTIONS

For ribs, season them with generously with spices. Place on a foil-lined cookie sheet, cover, and bake at 300 degrees for 2½–3 hours. Remove from oven and place on BBQ on high heat to crisp the outside.

In a medium saucepan, combine the first six ingredients and mix well. Add the remaining ingredients and heat thoroughly. Brush ribs with warm BBQ sauce.

AND HOMEMADE FRIES & FRY SAUCE

INGREDIENTS

CREAMY COLE SLAW

1 head green cabbage, thinly sliced

1 cup grated carrots

1 cup mayonnaise

1 cup crushed pineapple

2 Tbsp. apple cider vinegar

1½ tsp. yellow mustard

 INSTRUCTIONS

Mix all wet ingredients together. Pour over veggies and mix well.

INGREDIENTS

TANGY VINEGAR SLAW

½ head green cabbage, thinly sliced

½ head purple cabbage, thinly sliced

1 cup grated carrots

¾ cup olive oil

½ cup apple cider vinegar

¼ cup sugar

1 tsp. Real Salt

1 tsp. pepper

1 cup roasted salted sunflower seeds

 INSTRUCTIONS

Mix oil, vinegar, sugar, and spices together. Pour over veggies and mix well. Spread sunflower seeds over the finished slaw.

INGREDIENTS

HOMEMADE FRENCH FRIES
6 large russet potatoes
coconut oil

INSTRUCTIONS

Wash potatoes. Using a French fry cutter or a mandolin, cut potatoes into fry shape. Heat oil to 315–350 degrees. Fry potatoes until golden brown.

INGREDIENTS

PINK FRY SAUCE
½ cup mayonnaise
½ cup gluten-free ketchup
½ tsp. Real Salt
1 tsp. yellow mustard

YELLOW FRY SAUCE
½ cup mayonnaise
4 Tbsp. yellow mustard

INSTRUCTIONS

Combine all ingredients and mix well.

Filter out any small pieces and save your oil in a separate container to use again for French fries. We use ours a few times before discarding.

AMERICAN FLAG

COOKIE PIZZA

Anyone who has enjoyed a fruit pizza knows how addicting they are. The soft, sweet sugar cookie crust combined with the smooth, cool texture of the cream cheese topping is perfectly balanced in flavor by the tart, fresh fruit. This gluten-free version is perfect for your 4th of July celebration and is sure to be a crowd pleaser. —Chandice

INGREDIENTS

½ cup brown rice flour

½ cup sorghum flour

1 cup almond flour

1 cup potato starch

1 cup tapioca starch

1 cup white rice flour—
Bob's Red Mill only

1 cup butter

1 cup powdered sugar

1 tsp. baking soda

2 tsp. baking powder

2 tsp. xanthan gum

2 tsp. gluten-free vanilla extract

1 egg

1 cup sour cream

1 (8-oz.) pkg. cream cheese

⅓ cup powdered sugar

½ tsp. gluten-free vanilla extract

1 cup halved strawberries

½ cup blueberries

 INSTRUCTIONS

Preheat oven to 375 degrees. Combine all of the dry ingredients together. In another bowl, cream the butter and 1 cup powdered sugar together, and then add the sour cream, egg, and 2 teaspoons vanilla. Make sure not to over blend.

Slowly add in the dry ingredients one cup at a time, making sure to scrape down the sides of bowl after each time. Once mixed, gather the dough and roll out onto a pizza stone. Bake at 375 degrees for 10–12 minutes. In a bowl, combine the cream cheese with the remaining powdered sugar and vanilla extract. Spread over the cooled cookie crust and top with strawberries and blueberries following the design of an American flag.

SPOOKY SANDWICHES

AND CARAMEL CORN

Holidays are a big deal in our homes. My mom's mom made them really fun and full of tradition before she passed away and so my mom continued the love of holidays and tradition into how she raised us kids. Whether we were celebrating Valentine's or Halloween, I could count on a delicious themed meal. Kids absolutely love these spooky sandwiches, and who doesn't love caramel corn, right? —Chandice

INGREDIENTS

SPOOKY SANDWICHES

1 pkg. gluten-free hot dogs

1 pkg. gluten-free hot dog buns (optional)

1 cup gluten-free BBQ sauce (p. 202)

 INSTRUCTIONS

Slice the hot dogs into long strips. Fry the strips for 3–5 minutes stirring well and making sure they get some color. Add the barbecue sauce and cook an additional 1–2 minutes. Enjoy alone or fill gluten-free hot dog buns with them and serve.

INGREDIENTS

CARAMEL CORN

4 quarts air-popped, unbuttered popcorn

1 (14-oz.) can sweetened con-densed milk

1 cup honey

½ cup butter

2 cup brown sugar

1 Tbsp. gluten-free vanilla extract

 INSTRUCTIONS

Combine all ingredients in a large stockpot and cook on low heat until a candy thermometer reads 240 degrees or when cold water is dropped in, it forms a ball. Pour slowly over your popcorn and stir until all popcorn is covered.

NO. 216 GREEN BEAN CASSEROLE

WITH HOMEMADE FRIED ONIONS

We both love green bean casserole on Thanksgiving Day. It just isn't the same without it. There are no gluten-free fried onions in the grocery store so we got creative and made them on our own. They were so delicious that we now use them in a number of other things we make for our families. One thing to remember, do not use purple onions ... they look kind of worm-like, and your kids may call you out on it. We fill our dedicated gluten-free deep fryer with coconut oil then change the oil only a few times a year, as we don't do many fried things. It is an investment at first but you will find that the oil can be used many times over again. —Chandice

INGREDIENTS

14 oz. cream of chicken soup (page 80)

1 tsp. gluten-free soy sauce

4 (15-oz.) cans green beans, drained (or use fresh or frozen)

1 tsp. black pepper

1⅓ cups gluten-free fried onions

FRIED ONIONS

coconut oil for frying

2 large onion

¼ cup brown rice flour

¼ cup tapioca starch

¼ cup white rice flour

¼ cup potato starch

1 tsp. black pepper

1 tsp. Real Salt, plus more for seasoning

1 cup milk

INSTRUCTIONS

Slice onions into thin rings, and then soak in milk. Combine flours, Real Salt, and pepper. Heat oil in a large skillet or your deep fryer. Remove a few onion rings from milk and coat in flour. Fry in oil. Drain and sprinkle with a little more Real Salt to your liking.

Combine green beans, soup, gluten-free soy sauce, pepper, and ⅔ cup fried onions in a casserole dish. Bake 25 minutes at 350 degrees. Sprinkle with remaining fried onions and bake 5 more minutes.

CANDIED SWEET

POTATOES

This is another Thanksgiving recipe that we can't live without. We aren't your typical marshmallow topped sweet potato people. We only enjoy it when the inside is creamy and the top is sweet and a bit crunchy like this recipe. —Chandice

INGREDIENTS

2 large sweet potatoes, mashed

1 (14-oz.) can sweetened condensed milk

½ cup brown sugar

2 eggs

¼ cup butter

1 tsp. gluten-free vanilla

dash of Real Salt

TOPPING

½ cup brown sugar

½ cup chopped pecans

⅛ cup brown rice flour

⅛ cup tapioca starch

2 Tbsp. cold butter

INSTRUCTIONS

Combine all ingredients and spread into an 8 × 8 dish.

In another bowl, combine topping ingredients with your hands until mixed together but still crumbly and sprinkle over the top. Bake at 325 degrees for 45 minutes.

APPLE

TANA'S
TIPS
TAKE IT UP A NOTCH

Step it up a notch in this recipe and replace regular white sugar with coconut palm sugar. Coconut palm sugar has a lower glycemic impact so it is less likely to spike your blood sugar and it will give your apple filling a hint of caramel that, combined with cinnamon, is absolutely delicious.

PIE

Apple pie is an American classic and now you can make this classic in a delicious gluten-free version. With fresh apples and a pie crust that won't fall apart, but is still light and flaky, even the most discerning pie connoisseur won't know it's gluten-free! —Tana

INGREDIENTS

**pastry for double-crust pie
(page 224)**

APPLE PIE FILLING

**6–8 apples, peeled, cored, and
thinly sliced (I like using Granny
Smith apples, but any will work)**

1 Tbsp. lemon juice

¾ cup sugar

¼ cup cornstarch

1 tsp. cinnamon

¼ tsp. nutmeg

2 Tbsp. butter

 INSTRUCTIONS

Preheat oven to 350 degrees. Prepare apples and toss with lemon juice to prevent browning. Pat dry with a paper towel. Add sugar, cornstarch, cinnamon, and nutmeg; toss to coat apples. Lay out a long piece of plastic wrap, wrapping over counter edge. Shape half of pie dough into a round disc. Sprinkle very lightly with white rice flour. Begin rolling, moving in a circular pattern at all angles to achieve a nice circular pie crust. Roll out bottom pastry to slightly larger than pie plate. Lift plastic and turn onto pie plate; readjust as necessary (Yes! You can adjust as needed with this pie crust!)

Fill with apple mixture, making a higher center with apples. Dot the top of apples with butter. Roll out top crust in the same manner as bottom and cover pie. Roll overhang edges of bottom crust onto the top crust to make a nice high edge.

Crimp edges using the tines of a fork or your fingers to make a fluted edge. Cut a few decorative steam vents into pie top. Brush a tablespoon or two of heavy whipping cream on the pie center (don't brush edges). Sprinkle additional sugar on top. Bake for 45–50 minutes.

PECAN

PIE

Maybe you've never tried a slice of gooey pecan pie. It is traditionally a Southern pie. After trying this pie you might decide you want to make it regularly, no matter what region of the country you're from. Many pecan pie recipes call for corn syrup, but we are taking this one up a notch by using pure maple syrup. It truly makes a world of difference. —Tana

INGREDIENTS

½ pastry crust recipe (page 224)
4 eggs
1 cup maple syrup
6 Tbsp. butter, melted
¾ cup sugar
¼ tsp. Real Salt
1 cup pecans

 INSTRUCTIONS

Preheat oven to 350 degrees. Using a stand mixer, whisk together eggs, syrup, butter, sugar and salt. Pour mixture into an unbaked pie shell. Add pecans spreading them evenly over the pie filling or make a decorative pattern with them. Bake for 40–50 minutes, until a toothpick in center comes out clean.

TANA'S
TIPS
TAKE IT UP A NOTCH

You can take this up a notch further by switching out the sugar for coconut palm sugar. I promise you will not mind the difference; in fact, you might really enjoy the soft caramel undertones it adds.

CHERRY PIE

I started making pie when I began working in a restaurant at 13 years old. I love pie and I love making a crust that is flaky and tender. Over the years I became very good at pie making. Then came gluten-free … I tried every recipe I came across and every mix I could find but I was not able to find anything with the desired taste and texture that really a good pie crust should have. How could I live with pie crusts being pieced together and crusts that crumbled when barely touched? I knew I couldn't, and since no one had come up with a really good gluten-free pie crust, I was determined I would. You can imagine my joy (as a pie lover) when I came up with a recipe that is every bit as good as a gluten pie crust. You truly cannot tell the different in the flavor and texture. You can roll it and work it just like real pie crust…sigh! Go ahead, make a beautiful lattice top or a turnover; now you can. All this and it's still light, flaky, and tender, just like real pie crust. (Did I already say that? Well it's worth saying again and maybe even again before I'm done!)

Everyone who has tried this crust has said that they would have never guessed it was gluten-free. One friend told me it was better than any regular crust he had eaten. Another friend said it was every bit as good as the regular pie crust her grandma used to make. One friend gave a piece of my pie to her husband and he said, "Are you sure this is from Tana, because this is not a gluten-free pie crust." I used to be the pie maker for Thanksgiving, but since going gluten-free and only making gluten-free pie crusts, other family members have started making pies with regular crusts. They have informed me that they are no longer worried about having pies with regular crusts at Thanksgiving, they like this crust so much they are fine eating my gluten-free pies. I can be the pie maker again! I am so excited (hard to tell, right?) about this stellar gluten-free pie crust and I'm so happy to share it with you. Oh, by the way, the cherry pie filling is really good too. —Tana

INGREDIENTS

CHERRY PIE FILLING

3 lb. cherries (frozen or fresh, pitted)

1 cup sugar

⅓ cup cornstarch

1–2 drops gluten-free almond extract (optional)

STELLAR PASTRY CRUST

½ cup brown rice flour

1 cup white rice flour

1 cup tapioca starch

½ cup arrowroot starch

1 tsp. xanthan gum

1 tsp. gelatin

1 tsp. Real Salt

1 Tbsp. buttermilk powder

2 Tbsp. sugar

1 cup butter, frozen

2 Tbsp. buttermilk

1 egg, beaten

1 Tbsp. apple cider vinegar

3½–4 Tbsp. ice water

WITH LATTICE TOP

 INSTRUCTIONS

For the filling, in a large sauté pan or skillet combine all ingredients and mix well. On a medium heat cook the cherries until the mixture has thickened. Cool cherries before adding to unbaked pie crust.

For the crust, this recipe will work best with a stand mixer. Remove butter from freezer. Combine the first nine dry ingredients, mix well. Grate butter ½ cube at a time into dry ingredients. Lightly fluff in butter as you go. After all the butter is grated in, mix a few turns until all butter is coated in the flour mixture.

Add buttermilk, egg, and vinegar with a stir or two in between each one. Add ice water one tablespoon at a time. Mix together until dough sticks together and is a nice smooth texture. Roll out dough immediately or place in refrigerator. Dough should be slightly colder than room temperature when you roll it out, but not refrigerator cold. Dough will keep for a day or two in the refrigerator, but let it warm a little before using it.

Place plastic wrap on the counter surface with the end coming down over the countertop edge to help hold it tightly in place. With your hands, shape half of the dough into a slightly flattened disc shape and place on plastic wrap. Dust top of dough with a very small amount of white rice flour. Roll out dough working in a circular motion to achieve a nicely rounded pie crust which is slightly larger than your pie plate. After dough is rolled to the desired size, lift the plastic wrap with the dough on it and invert into the pie plate. Reposition as needed and remove plastic wrap. Plastic wrap will remove cleanly. I would say mend any broken pieces, but I doubt you will have any!

Fill pie crust with filling. Get a new piece of plastic wrap and repeat the process for the top crust. If you are making a lattice top, roll your top crust as directed. When you have reached the desired size, start cutting strips with either a lattice crust wheel (this will make a scalloped edge—you can get this for $4 or so at a cooking store) or a pizza cutting wheel (this will give you straight edges). Place the smaller pieces on the edges and the longer pieces in the middle. Do not cut off the over-hang; just fold it into itself to make a nice high edge and crimp the edges to seal using your favorite decorative pattern, such as fluting or using the tines of a fork. Brush a tiny bit of heavy cream on the top for deeper browning, avoiding the edges (this isn't necessary) and sprinkle with sugar to finish your pies off beautifully.

Bake at 400 degrees for approximately 30 minutes or until crust is golden brown. For single, unfilled crust, bake for about 20 minutes.

N⁰ 228

COCONUT CREAM

TANA'S TIPS TAKE IT UP A NOTCH

Make sure to check the label on your coconut extract; many contain grain alcohols. Distillation generally removes any gluten, but if you are very sensitive, select an extract that is free of grain alcohols.

PIE

Coconut cream pie looks like a special occasion dessert, but it is so easy you can make it any old time. I told a friend I was making homemade pudding and she said, "Oh, I make it all the time"; my comment was, "Not Jell-O pudding," and she said, "Can you do that, I mean make it completely from scratch?" Making your own homemade pudding makes this pie extra rich and creamy; it certainly will impress. —Tana

INGREDIENTS

Pastry crust recipe (page 224)

FILLING

3 cups whole milk, divided

3 cups whipping cream

3 Tbsp. butter

1 cup sugar

6 egg yolks

⅓ cup sugar

½ cup cornstarch

1 tsp. gluten-free coconut extract

1 cup coconut flakes

⅓ cup toasted coconut

whipped cream

INSTRUCTIONS

Divide dough in half and roll out each half and place in two 9-inch pie pans. Bake at 400 degrees for 20 minutes or until edges are lightly browned.

Place milk, cream, 1 cup sugar, and butter in a heavy saucepan or a double boiler. Cook until butter is melted and milk is slightly scalded.

Whisk together egg yolks and ⅓ cup sugar. Slowly add this mixture to the hot mixture, whisking lightly. Continue cooking for 10–15 minutes on a low heat until mixture starts to thicken a bit. Mix reserved milk and cornstarch together. Add to the hot milk mixture, whisking constantly. Intermittently whisk as mixture continues to cook for the next 5–10 minutes.

When pudding has thickened, blend in coconut extract. Remove from heat and stir in coconut. Pour filling into pie shells. Cover with plastic wrap (to avoid skimming) and place in refrigerator to cool. When cooled, top with whipped cream and toasted coconut.

CHRISTMAS EVE TRADITIONS:

Making and decorating gingerbread men on Christmas Eve is a tradition that many families enjoy, including ours. We love to pair the spicy, sweet cookies with rich homemade eggnog and hot cocoa for a truly delectable treat that will no doubt have you dreaming of sugarplums. —Chandice

INGREDIENTS

GINGERBREAD MEN

6 Tbsp. softened butter

1 cup sugar

1 cup molasses

1 egg

1 tsp. white vinegar

⅔ cup brown rice flour

⅔ cup sorghum flour

⅔ cup almond flour

1 cup tapioca starch

1 cup potato starch

2 Tbsp. coconut flour

½ tsp. cream of tartar

1½ tsp. xanthan gum OR baking powder

2 tsp. ginger

1¼ tsp. baking soda

1 Tbsp. allspice

¼ tsp. Real Salt

 INSTRUCTIONS

In a bowl beat the butter and sugar. Mix in molasses, egg, and vinegar. In another bowl, combine the flour and all dry ingredients. Gradually add the dry mixture to the creamed mixture. Cover and refrigerate for a minimum of 4 hours and up to overnight. On a white rice or gluten-free starch floured surface, roll the dough out to ¼ of an inch thick.

Dust your cookie cutters with gluten-free flour or starch then cut the rolled out dough into shapes. Using a gluten-free floured or starched metal spatula gently place the cookies on a baking sheet at least 1 inch apart. Bake at 375 degrees for 12–14 minutes.

GINGERBREAD MEN, EGGNOG, AND HOT COCOA

INGREDIENTS

RICH HOT COCOA

2 cup whipping cream

¾ cup milk chocolate chips

2 tsp. gluten-free vanilla extract

½ cup powdered sugar

 INSTRUCTIONS

Combine all ingredients in a saucepan and whisk over low heat until well combined, smooth and hot. Top with prepared whipping cream and more chocolate chips or shaved dark chocolate.

INGREDIENTS

SMOOTH AND CREAMY EGGNOG

½ gallon milk

1 pint whipping cream

6 egg yolks

1 cup sugar

1 tsp. nutmeg

2 tsp. cinnamon

2 tsp. gluten-free vanilla extract

 INSTRUCTIONS

Whisk together the milk and egg yolks. Bring to a low boil then add the remaining ingredients. Let cool a bit, then store in your refrigerator and serve chilled.

BELGIAN

WAFFLES

Getting the right mixture to achieve a light and fluffy waffle gluten-free can be a challenge. These waffles really did it for me; they are so delicious! Nice and soft on the inside and lightly crispy on the outside, they will quickly become the most requested "special breakfast" for occasions such as Christmas morning, Easter brunch, and birthdays. —Tana

INGREDIENTS

⅓ cup almond flour

⅓ cup brown rice flour

⅓ cup sorghum flour

½ cup tapioca starch

⅓ cup potato starch

1 Tbsp. coconut flour

1 Tbsp. baking powder

½ tsp. Real Salt

¼ cup sugar

3 eggs, separated

½ cup butter, melted

1 cup milk

1 Tbsp. gluten-free vanilla

 INSTRUCTIONS

Heat waffle iron. In a stand mixer, combine egg yolks and sugar; mix together. Melt butter, and then add milk and vanilla. Combine milk and egg mixtures.

Combine the first eight dry ingredients; add a little at a time to the wet mixture until well blended. Whip reserved egg whites until soft peaks form. Fold into batter, without over mixing.

Oil hot waffle iron. Using an ice cream scoop or metal measuring cup, place a heaping ½ cup of batter in center of waffle iron. Use the back of the scoop or cup and spread batter outward. Close iron and cook according to manufacturer's directions. Top with syrup, powdered sugar, or whipped cream and berries.

TANA'S
TIPS
TAKE IT UP A NOTCH

Maple sugar is a great sweetener that is less processed than plain white sugar. Try switching it out for the sugar in this recipe. As a nice touch it will add a hint of maple to these yummy waffles, and the aroma is sure to rouse your sleepy heads from their beds.

CUPCAKES

Designer cupcakes have become all the rage. The prices are high and there is no end to the variety and mounds of frosting upon them. Make your own designer cupcakes at home and save a ton. We should start with the basics, a buttery soft yellow cupcake with an amazing chocolate frosting. Even basic can go designer. I made these cupcakes for my son's birthday this year and they were a huge hit. When party time was over there wasn't a cupcake left in sight. This might not be surprising if it was a party for undiscerning 5 year olds. But my son is 23, so the party was nearly all adults—very finicky adults, I might add. —Tana

INGREDIENTS

YELLOW CUPCAKE

⅔ cups brown rice flour

¼ cup sorghum flour

⅔ cups white rice flour

⅔ cups tapioca starch

⅔ cups potato starch

2 Tbsp. coconut flour

1 tsp. xanthan gum

1 tsp. gelatin

1 Tbsp. baking powder

¼ tsp. baking soda

⅛ tsp. cream of tartar

½ tsp. Real Salt

1¾ cups sugar

½ cup butter

¼ cup coconut oil

1 tsp. gluten-free vanilla

6 eggs, separated

1 cup sour cream

¾ cup milk

CREAMY CHOCOLATE FROSTING

1 cup butter, softened

4 Tbsp. heavy cream

2 tsp. gluten-free vanilla

½ cup cacao powder

3 cups powdered sugar

INSTRUCTIONS

Preheat oven to 350 degrees. Using a stand mixer, cream together butter, coconut oil, and sugar. Add vanilla, egg yolks, sour cream, and milk, and blend well. Combine all remaining dry ingredients and mix well. Mix dry ingredients into wet ingredients a cup at a time. Mix until well blended. Whip egg whites until stiff peaks form. Fold into cake batter. Using a small scoop, scoop batter into a muffin tin lined with cupcake liners. Fill to ¾ full. Bake for 20–22 minutes, until lightly browned and dome springs back. Let cupcakes cool slightly, remove from muffin tin, and continue cooling on a wire rack.

In a stand mixer with the whisk attachment, blend together butter, sugar, and cacao powder. Add vanilla and cream, and continue mixing until smooth and fluffy. Using a piping bag or a ziplock bag with a corner snipped, pipe frosting on cooled cupcakes. Add any additional topping desired.

ACKNOWLEDGMENTS

I would like to first thank my wonderful husband who not only supports me in anything I do but also literally helps make my dreams a reality. Without him and his super sweet web development skills, Gluten-free Frenzy and Gluten-free Calendar wouldn't exist. Thank you for all the last-minute requests, taste testing, and really everything, hun; you are my best friend and I feel honored to be your wife for eternity. PLUS, you make one mean batch of gluten-free fried chicken!

Thank you to my children for encouraging Mommy to try new recipes and for being both positive and honest when I needed it. Thank you for being adventurous and going to ethnic restaurants with me on our little dates, because we all know Daddy won't go. I can't imagine my life without you sweet angel babies. Thank you for giving me the greatest gift imaginable: being your mother.

Though I am writing this book with my mom, it wouldn't seem right not to thank her. Because of her positivity and enthusiasm for gluten-free cooking, I was able to take my diagnosis and find the best in it from day one. I can't imagine a greater mother in the world. Even when I was a pain-in-the-neck teenager, you and Dad were always there cheering me on in my successes. Thanks, Dad, for always providing your family with spiritual guidance and a place to call home, not only physically but also in your heart. You are our hero.

I love that I have a big wonderful family but it would make for a very long list of individual thanks so I would like to say thank you collectively for the role you have each had in my life's journey. I know it is because of the wonderful family that I have been blessed with that I am here today. I couldn't ask for better people to be surrounded by.

I am so thankful for my Arizona sisters and the support they provided me during this cookbook writing process. They listened to more about gluten-free living than I am sure they ever wanted to hear but did it with enthusiasm. From being at my events and helping with my kids to taping my TV segments and giving me constructive criticism, you guys have been more of a support to me than I deserve. For that and for giving me friendship that will last forever, I thank you.

To all my GFFs, or gluten-free friends, I want to thank you for the camaraderie you provide in this community. You are amazing and I admire each of you so much! Tammy, my mom and I both want to especially thank you for inspiring us to do this cookbook and for providing us with priceless suggestions and advice. You are our favorite cookbook author without a doubt!

Thank you to all you wonderful readers of Gluten-free Frenzy and for all your stories, comments, and support. I feel so lucky to have the greatest online support. Thank you to the national celiac organizations, especially the Celiac Disease Foundation for all you have done for me and our community. To all the wonderful companies and fantastic bloggers out there that I have had the privilege of working with,

I feel so blessed to associate with and know you! Thank you Jordan and Vanessa at Delight Gluten-free Magazine for giving me a wonderful magazine to write for. I am honored to be a part of your team. To the team at 3TV Your Life A to Z, thank you for allowing me to be a regular contributor on the show and have my dream of teaching gluten-free living and information on celiac disease to the masses a reality. It was such a fun ride!

Thank you to the good folks at Cedar Fort Publishing for seeing our vision and for believing in us. Hannah, thank you so much for being with us from day one and for making our ideas come to life. You have been pivotal in this writing process and we thank you for that and for your continual kindness and enthusiasm.

Finally, I am so thankful to my Heavenly Father and Savior Jesus Christ everyday for opening doors for me to share the knowledge that I have learned and meet the most amazing people along the way. I feel beyond blessed to have been given this life.

CHANDICE PROBST

I would like to thank my amazing husband. He has always been supportive and positive about the lifestyle and menu changes he has made along with me. I love that he is always willing to taste test my new creations and for his excitement when it turns out great. He is an incredible husband and father. He is my best friend and my knight in shining armor. I'm glad you are mine forever.

I would also like to thank each of my amazing children. Over the years they have rarely complained about anything (food) that was placed before them. We have made many drastic changes in what's for dinner and they are always good sports about it. I love each of them, their spouses, and my grandchildren dearly. They are the joy of my life. All this cooking would be for nothing without them (and Jim). Chandice and I have had an especially wonderful time working on this cookbook together. She never ceases to amaze me with all her gifts and talents and the wonderful woman that she is. I am glad we are not only mother and daughter but really good friends too.

I am also thankful for my extended family for always being there for me and always being there to eat my food. I am blessed to have so many great people in my life. I am also blessed to have had wonderful parents who taught me important life lessons.

It is wonderful to work where you have good friends. I would like to thank my Real Foods Market foodie friends for their support and their shared joy in good food. And for the good folks at Redmond who are supportive and always willing to try my food. Especially for Brent Haddock who was so helpful and shot great cover photos for me.

I appreciate Hannah and Cedar Fort Publishing and their excitement in helping us share our delectable gluten-free recipes with all of you.

I am eternally grateful for my Lord and Savior Jesus Christ and my Father in Heaven for the faith they bring into my life, for the blessing of love and family and for a knowledge of truth.

TANA BESENDORFER

COOKING MEASUREMENT EQUIVALENTS

Cups	Tablespoons	Fluid Ounces
⅛ cup	2 Tbsp.	1 fl. oz.
¼ cup	4 Tbsp.	2 fl. oz.
⅓ cup	5 Tbsp. + 1 tsp.	
½ cup	8 Tbsp.	4 fl. oz.
⅔ cup	10 Tbsp. + 2 tsp.	
¾ cup	12 Tbsp.	6 fl. oz.
1 cup	16 Tbsp.	8 fl. oz.

Cups	Fluid Ounces	Pints/Quarts/Gallons
1 cup	8 fl. oz.	½ pint
2 cups	16 fl. oz.	1 pint = ½ quart
3 cups	24 fl. oz.	1½ pints
4 cups	32 fl. oz.	2 pints = 1 quart
8 cups	64 fl. oz.	2 quarts = ½ gallon
16 cups	128 fl. oz.	4 quarts = 1 gallon

Other Helpful Equivalents

1 Tbsp.	3 tsp.
8 oz.	½ lb.
16 oz.	1 lb.

METRIC MEASUREMENT EQUIVALENTS

Approximate Weight Equivalents

Ounces	Pounds	Grams
4 oz.	¼ lb.	113 g
5 oz.		142 g
6 oz.		170 g
8 oz.	½ lb.	227 g
9 oz.		255 g
12 oz.	¾ lb.	340 g
16 oz.	1 lb.	454 g

Approximate Volume Equivalents

Cups	US Fluid Ounces	Milliliters
⅛ cup	1 fl. oz.	30 ml
¼ cup	2 fl. oz.	59 ml
½ cup	4 fl. oz.	118 ml
¾ cup	6 fl. oz.	177 ml
1 cup	8 fl. oz.	237 ml

Other Helpful Equivalents

½ tsp.	2½ ml
1 tsp.	5 ml
1 Tbsp.	15 ml

INDEX

ABOUT CHANDICE

Chandice is the founder of the popular website www.glutenfreefrenzy.com, which is known as the #1 gluten-free giveaway site and provides individuals with recipes, reviews, giveaways, and much more. She is co-founder and CEO of Gluten-free Calendar, which hosts Celebrate Celiac™ events and Celiac Awareness Nights with professional athletic teams nationwide to promote celiac awareness, raise proceeds for non-profit research facilities, and achieve the company's slogan of Unity in the Gluten-free Community™.

Chandice founded the Celiac Disease Foundation Arizona East Valley Chapter in 2009 and enjoyed serving as the president for four years. She has a Bachelors of Science in exercise and health wellness from Arizona State University and graduated with magna cum laude honors. Recently she joined the Delight Gluten-free Magazine team as a regular contributing writer and is also an Expert Among Us writer for SheKnows.com. Chandice has been featured on ABC 15 Sonoran Living, Channel 12 Arizona Midday, and in print publications *Women's World*, *The Arcadian Journal*, and *Total Kid Magazine*. She was a regular contributor on Channel 3 Your Life A to Z in Arizona for over a year as their gluten-free guru before her family made the move to St. George, Utah. In her spare time, she also teaches gluten-free cooking classes and seminars and enjoys being a guest speaker nationwide at different gluten-free expos and events.

In addition to her above professions, Chandice considers her role as a wife, mother, and everyday cook to her family to be of greatest value.

ABOUT TANA

Tana has been a passionate cook since the age of 11. She got her first job at her hometown restaurant, Mom's Café, making pies. Tana is known by all who associate with her as one of the greatest cooks. She is a foodie with focus on health and nutrition to heal the body. Tana is currently a buyer for Real Foods Market where she seeks out the best products to be featured in these one-of-a-kind stores. Her greatest passion is still cooking with and for her family. She especially loves making the holidays more enjoyable for everyone with themed, nutritious food that would put a smile on anyone's face. Friends of the family often congregate at her home just to enjoy her "famous" cooking.